The
Free
Mind

The Free Mind

also by Robert Powell

Zen and Reality

Crisis in Consciousness

The Inward Path to Liberation

Robert Powell

The Julian Press, Inc. New York

Acknowledgment is made to *The Aryan Path* and *The Middle Way* for material in this book which first appeared in those magazines.

The quotations in Chapter 11 of this book from J. Krishnamurti's *First and Last Freedom* and his Madras and Paris Talks are by kind permission of Krishnamurti Writings, Inc., Ojai, California.

Contents

Contents

Foreword

The miscellaneous essays, talks, and correspondence that comprise this volume all center around the crucial issue of freedom. What, in this connection, is meant by "freedom"? Ask ten different people what the word means to them, and very likely each will come up with a different definition. Most of these will be descriptions of partial freedoms, that is, political freedom, economic freedom, sexual freedom, freedom from hunger, from oppression, from pollution, and so forth, indicating a desire to be free from the various problems that beset us. They have been designated as "partial" because, however necessary they may be for human welfare—and as such they are crying out for immediate realization—there is a much more fundamental freedom which has to be brought about before human beings can realize their potential for true happiness and creativity.

Difficult though it may be for most people to accept, many of our social problems, which we are at present trying to solve piecemeal, could be eliminated at one fell swoop. How? Not through any political means—by replacing the radical right by the radical left, or vice versa—but by doing away with our present social structure, *because it is this in essence which is the cause of our plight.* To deal with the problems in their present setting would be like the symptomatic treatment of a serious disease; it can never lead to a state of health.

But, obviously, the majority of people still want things the way they are; otherwise they would have kicked out the system long ago. Such an event is not likely to occur, however, and for a very simple reason: the Society we have is the Society we deserve, since it basically reflects our own secret being. Violence, greed, corruption—they are there for everyone to see. Therefore, for Society to change it is necessary for Man to change—and that is the last thing he desires to do, although he may well pay lip service to it. For those of us, at present still in a minority, who *do* desire a complete change and can see the essential and inescapable logic of the world situation, the task is twofold. First and foremost, we must change ourselves individually, if a new Society is to come about in which human beings are truly free. In the meantime—and we cannot afford to wait until then, because the house is on fire—we must do all we can to press for reforms by whatever means, short of violence (both within the legal and political channels, and without), so that at least some of the hungry may be fed, some of the poor may be housed, and perhaps some fewer people may die unnecessarily.

So, there is a need for two kinds of action: one, a total revolution in the psyche, and the other, a change within the present social structure, which is the (partial) revolution for which many young people in different parts of the world are actively working. In this book we shall be concerned only with the first type of action; the second would be more suitably dealt with in a socioeconomic treatise.

The freedom which is the subject of this work is not a fragmentary thing, not a reaction against a particular set of circumstances that constrains us—in short, not a freedom *from* something or even from everything; but it is a release of the mind from its inherent bondage. We say "inherent" because, unknown to many, if man were given complete external freedom there still would be something within the mind itself to bind him; in other words, he would (continue to) create his own (internal) problems. That "something" has been variously described as "ego," "conditioning," "duality," and so forth. What we call it is of little importance, but what is significant—and this is one of the main objects of the present work—is to investigate whether it is at all possible for human beings to free themselves from within. The emphasis here lies on the word "investigate," for the author in no way claims to give out any teaching, old or new, nor does he provide any final answers to burning questions. Such a treatment would be altogether too simplistic. Where, nevertheless, he appears to do so, or where he seems to be somewhat overemphatic, this was done to stimulate thoughtfulness and further discussion. For in this business of living there can be no teachers and pupils—the absurdity of it, to teach others how to manage their lives!—but we are all learning together. Here, for once, there is a great chasm between "learning" and "being taught"; and if you think you are being taught, then you have not yet learned a thing.

Because, ultimately, each of us is completely alone and must act and learn from that state of "aloneness," it is heart-warming, and perhaps also fruitful, for many of us to exchange views about certain intensely personal and deeply felt issues—views frequently completely at variance with almost everything one reads and hears about. Is it that, when we find others have glimpsed something very similar, or identical, to the nature of our own insights, it gives us an indication that we are on the right road? And also, perhaps, that in this chaotic world we feel we belong to a brotherhood of man which transcends geographical origin, race, and conditioning?

Much of the correspondence the author receives testifies to a thirst for a more meaningful existence, a life that is more attuned to the unexpressed laws of nature than to the stated objectives of Society. Those who are so inclined are, whether they like it or not, necessarily deeply involved in the battle between the forces of conservatism and non-conformism, or "dissent," which rages over large areas of the globe. If one is loyal to the truth, one cannot be loyal to anything else; unwittingly, one is a radical of some kind, because truth itself is a most radical and explosive thing. This means living dangerously in more ways than one: it may well lead us into a direct clash with Authority in all its ugliness and brutality. And although a man at peace with himself does not think in terms of personal or factional antagonism and will never be the first to use brute force, such a confrontation may well unleash violence. Why? Simply because we live in a Society that is founded on, and maintained by, violence in various forms, some very

Foreword

obvious and others very subtle. Yet, there are those, mostly in positions of power and authority, who admonish others, less privileged, not to be violent—the rank hypocrisy of it!

Finally, in launching this work, the author would like to dedicate it to all those young minds, of any age, who are in active revolt against our present way of living, not merely because they feel frustrated in their desire for a sane and peaceful existence, but because they clearly perceive that Society, based as it is on utterly false values, is in dire need of being restructured fundamentally and totally.

R.P.

San Diego, California
August 1971

The
Free
Mind

Liberation
and
Duality

In the age-old quest for human liberation, two predominant patterns can be distinguished. In large areas of the East, the major concern has ever been with an inward liberation that assigned only secondary importance to the external, material world. This attitude has naturally tended to some kind of Quietism with respect to worldly activity, and so to a neglect of material living conditions.

In the West, the liberation of mankind has been pursued mainly in societal terms, that is, externally. Through improvement of physical conditions by means of a rapidly developing technology, and also by certain forms of so-called "enlightened" legislation, rulers have sought to provide "the greatest happiness to the greatest number of people"—even if the number that actually benefited was not always very great.

Neither of these extreme opposites in attitude is likely to bring about the optimal psychological climate for the liberation of consciousness. On the one hand, a hungry man will be too busy providing for his family and self to bother with his spiritual welfare—an empty stomach is not particularly conducive to meditation, although some people seem to think it is—and the struggle for physical survival in a hostile world will use up a great deal of energy that otherwise might have been available to the quest.

On the other hand, the individual striving to "better" himself in a materialistically oriented society is likely to get irretrievably lost in *that* quest. He, too, will divert a great amount of essential energy toward irrelevant goals, and in many cases he will not even know "what's it all about," having lost touch completely with the source of his being.

There is, however, a third approach with respect to the possibility of human deliverance, which is not merely a middle path or a compromise between the aforementioned approaches, but is in actual fact the negation of either. This Way has been recognized from times immemorial by individuals both in the East and in the West as the only feasible solution to the problem of human bondage. Very briefly, it rests on the fact that there is no division between the "inner" and the "outer," that what we call the "spiritual" life is actually none other than the everyday life, Life being indivisible. This means that the "inward turning" of the mind is a lopsided action unless it is accompanied by an examination of the corresponding outward phenomena. And similarly, to regulate the outer—for example, by legislating for peace, against racial discrimination, and so forth—without a corresponding change of heart, is an equally lopsided action. From this it follows that any kind of deliverance that

2

is not merely apparent, partial, or temporary must be a spontaneous process in which "will" plays no part whatsoever—a process that results only from a deep understanding of the whole field of conscious activity. Thus, the only true liberation is that of the man who lives fully and intensely in this world, without any mental reservations, although he may not be of it.

With such a strictly nondualistic approach toward Reality, a truly integrated way of life becomes possible in which everything, however apparently irrelevant, assumes a deeper significance. For example, fathoming the unsubstantiality of the atom may help in self-knowing, in looking with clear eyes into the corresponding emptiness of our self-nature. And conversely, knowing the self, the observer, may throw fresh light on the world, which, after all, becomes known only by mediation of the observer's senses. Also, according to this view, Society cannot be divorced from the individual, because politically, economically, and psychologically he is entirely the product of that Society. To ask which of the two is basically more real is very much like asking the proverbial question of the egg and the chicken.

Because to live is to act, and because every action directly affects the relationship with others and the entire environment, the man in search of emancipation is an involved man. The "religious" man who shuns every form of worldly activity because he is 100 percent of his time working for a personal salvation is as much an absurdity as the "worldly" person who spends all his time making money without ever doing anything that is not essentially "gainful." It is not even a question of balancing one's activities—say, mixing a certain amount of "meditation" with an equivalent amount of "do-gooding." The man who is true to himself, and therefore never conforms, is a disturbing factor to the dark forces of conservatism in the world, without even having to put himself out to "close down the government." Such a man, in the course of a lifetime, will have a tremendous effect upon society; and though perhaps only imperceptibly, will have contributed in a real way to change in that society.

In the following chapters the question of man's bondage and his relation to the world of phenomena will be examined from various angles. In the course of this inquiry we shall come upon certain signposts to the ultimate liberation. To emphasize the nondualistic nature of this reaching out for enlightenment, which may well be designated "man's true work," we have indicated that essentially there is neither the one nor the many, neither the self nor the world, neither matter nor mind—as opposed to, and separate from, one another; but that Reality is a unified field in which thought has created the manifold divisions and that it is within these same thought-created barriers that the mind is imprisoned. Thus, in examining social issues we have ever sought to reduce these to the idiosyncrasies of individual consciousness as it is presently molded, and in examining the conflicts in the individual psyche we have tried to show how they derive and are nurtured from the underlying social consciousness. Consequently, we believe that a search for meaning in any area of phenomenal existence, as long as it is on a sufficiently fundamental level, can bring man nearer to transcendence of the self.

Crisis

in

Consciousness

One need not be a very astute observer of mankind to see that human affairs all over the world are in a state of crisis. This crisis manifests itself in almost every sphere of activity —in politics, economics, religion, education, to mention only a few—and in a general feeling of confusion and restlessness. Some say what is happening today is the inevitable result of man's scientific capability having outgrown his moral development. Others say it is all due to the crowded living conditions in our big cities; yet others blame it on the so-called generation gap. In short, there appear to be almost as many explanations as there are problems.

This writer does not view the present crisis as a fortuitous coming together of various problems caused by a too rapidly advancing technology. Nor does he attribute it to the failure of any one political or economic system, or to the "population explosion." To him these are merely symptoms that something is basically wrong; they accentuate the crisis but do not cause it. He sees the crisis as being of an entirely different, much more fundamental, nature that finds its origin in the psyche of man—in other words, a crisis in consciousness. It is here where all our woes originate, and it is only here where the real solution to our difficulties can be effected.

Our present social structure is like a house built on an unsound foundation, because it is based on the troubled psychological state of the individual. The only proper cure is to haul down the structure and rebuild it on the right kind of foundation. This means that what is needed first and foremost is a complete change of heart in man. Only through such an individual transformation can there be a renewal of the psychological structure of Society—not the other way round. Once Society has renewed itself psychologically, it can easily take any problems in its stride; then, nothing will be impossible.

However, this entails nothing less than a tremendous inward revolution, a cleansing of the mind that comes about only through self-knowledge. At the same time, it must be realized that this is the only revolution. Any other so-called revolution, whether it be the Marxist Revolution or the Sexual Revolution, are relatively superficial changes that have not brought into being an essentially new way of life. This is because the inner always overcomes the outer; that is, a mere outward change is eventually always negated when man's inherent nature reasserts itself. By having so-called ideals, we think, the world will be changed. But, the "ideal" cannot stand up to reality and is essentially mean-

6

ingless. In fact, it is worse than that: it becomes a considerable hindrance, since it encourages an escape from Reality. To give a very simple example: almost everybody in this world talks about wanting peace; yet, most of us live with and accept war as though it were a most natural state —not the idiocy it is. This merely illustrates one aspect of the present crisis: as long as man is not at peace with himself, he creates an ugly, violent world. But the moment he is at one with himself, he brings about a peaceful world, which is the only way of achieving a decent, civilized Society.

Is Suffering Real or Illusory?

In the East there is an ancient philosophy which states that all phenomenal existence rests upon an illusion; that is, the world as perceived by the senses is not ultimately real. This philosophy, which now also has its followers in the West, is made the basis for an approach to human liberation. For, it is said, if the world is not real, then our problems and suffering are not real either; this simple realization should be sufficient to enable us to step out of sorrow immediately and easily.

This writer feels that, whatever may be the truth of the stated proposition, it is quite irrelevant to the matter of solving one's day-to-day problems. Merely to call the world "unreal"—even if it be so—does not make it disappear; in practice, it seems no easier to deal with a world so designated than to deal with the customary "real" world. In other words, what difference there may be between "real persons dealing with real problems in a real world" and

7

"unreal persons dealing with unreal problems in an unreal world" appears of merely academic interest. And in view of this, it could further be asked whether it still makes much sense to differentiate between these two postulated situations. Maybe, to ask whether the world is real or not was the wrong kind of question to begin with; for do we have any yardsticks by which to measure that reality or unreality? I feel that the question can never be resolved on these lines, because our "yardsticks" are ever part of this "world"; if the world were to be unreal, the yardsticks would be likewise: whatever answers they may provide would be meaningless.

The following analogy might be used to illustrate our predicament. To a man asleep, the dream world appears as real as does the waking world to the man who is awake. The former, so long as he is sleeping, has no means of determining the reality of his world (for all his yardsticks are dream entities, too). If he had, he would wake up at once. Just so, the man who is awake is in no position to test the reality of his waking world. It may well be that what appears to him as a state of wakefulness is in actual fact only another kind of dream.

We have dwelled upon this topic to some extent because it illustrates rather well the elusiveness of absolute knowledge as well as the impotence of speculative philosophy in embracing reality. But, it seems to me, such an exercise as we have been doing, which might be called meditative contemplation, is not entirely negative in its effects. For out of it comes a further realization, namely, that the mind itself, as the instrument of logic or discursive thought, is ever limited by its own inherent nature; it exists, as it were, within a vacuum, a void, which is what *is*. Yet, on a deeper level, it is also in itself no different from that Void: it only *appears*, in its Suchness, to be different from that which is No-Mind. Any problem which the mind presents to itself, any question which it poses to itself, is like a circular argument: the answer is already implicit in the formulation of the question.

It is the mind that has created this problem as to the reality of the world; and since it is seen that the mind, this fragile consciousness which can only be active within its own conditioning, is a totally relative entity, naturally whatever thought concludes is meaningless in terms of ultimate or absolute knowledge. To put this somewhat differently, the ultimate certainty that it can attain is ever of the same order as the certainty that is obtained in a dream: because we now realize that our waking existence—this endless stream of thought and sense impressions—is only another dream. And to say, as some apparently do, that the postulate of the world's relativity already implies the existence, somewhere, of its opposite, an absolute world, is now seen to be false too: the world which we conceive is neither absolute nor relative, neither real nor unreal, for each of these designations is mind-made and therefore ultimately irrelevant when it comes to dealing with No-Mind.

Now what happens if one has come thus far, and has seen that whatever answer thought arrives at has no validity whatsoever? Does not the mind become completely silent, not through compulsion, but of its own accord, because it is perceived that every movement of thought, every form of speculation, leads to further illusion and digression? One has completely rejected religious doctrine; one has denied authority, both outward and inward; and one is no longer concerned with metaphysical formulations. And most importantly, the duality of mind which has given rise to the debate over the reality of the world is seen to be the very cause of all conflict and mental suffering. Then, out of that state of silence, from that void, the mind emerges wonderfully fresh, clear, and concentrated in the present. There is the realization that no spiritual life exists apart from the everyday life, that there are no absolutes to be pursued, yet that the problems of the world are very real indeed. To work diligently toward their solution, as one meets them— without thought of one's success or failure—*is* the (only) practice of the spiritual life. And in that, if one does it, will it not be found to hold a clue to our happiness?

About the Inward Aspect of Everyday Affairs

Most of us seek to escape from our pressing psychological problems rather than to solve them. We have so many ways in which we can escape: through drugs, through innumerable forms of amusement, through organized religion— which is both a form of amusement and an opiate—and through philosophy—which is a mildly amusing form of intellectual divertissement. And if we do not escape, we look toward guidance and support, for we need moral crutches even more than we need those of the physical variety. Unfortunately or fortunately, however, there exists an area in everyone's life where one is completely alone; on that level we have to fight our own battles, face our innermost anxieties and our immaturity so that we may mature. If we don't do it ourselves, who can help us? After all, that is what life is all about, is it not?—a continuous learning process, which is something entirely different from the idea

10

that "having been told, we have learned something." If you are told how to direct your life, how to solve a particular psychological problem, life will always frustrate your neat little blueprint by presenting you with fresh problems about which you have not been told. Then, you will need ever more help, more external support, and therefore you will never be able to stand on your own feet.

This writer is certainly not going to further this process. His statements are not to be lapped up as gospel truth, but are meant to provoke the reader to think the issue out for himself. Merely to accept or reject has no value whatsoever; it leaves the problem basically unresolved. But to deepen our understanding it may be useful just to discuss, to inquire together, to highlight certain interesting facts (*not* opinions) which one has discovered for oneself—without any pressure, any desire to make others accept a certain point of view. The facts (if they *are* facts) will speak for themselves; in fact, *only* the facts can do so. Therefore, one of the first necessities will be to be able to differentiate between fact and mere opinion. My so-called "fact" may well be an opinion, and the sooner I realize it the better. And my fact, being a fact, may well be an opinion to you. To be open to facts, to be accurate in one's observations, and to see clearly the false as the false, needs a certain sensitivity and a great amount of passion—a passion to perceive and live by the Truth for the sake of that Truth. Let us hope that our joint inquiry into many burning questions may awaken such sensitivity and bring about a passionate spirit of inquiry in both the reader and the writer.

It seems to me that what many thoughtful people in the world desire is a deepening of their understanding of fundamental issues; they are beginning to realize that ignorance thereof is one of the main causes of their frustration. Also, the truth slowly appears to dawn that for such basic understanding one need not go to books, teachers, and religious revelations—none of which can be trusted and all of which are open to varying interpretations. Nor is one to be palmed off with a belief, which is really a form of solace but which has nothing whatsoever to do with what *is*.

What we will attempt to do in this work is to discuss human problems of general interest from a more "inward" point of view than is customary. This statement needs further elucidating. A problem, whether it be of the individual or of society, can never be solved in isolation. For example, the problem of war cannot be properly understood without understanding the fragmentation of mankind into nationalities, religions, races. The problem of love can never be understood without going into the whole question of relationship. Beneath the superficial aspects of a problem lies the tremendous turmoil in Consciousness which is, as it were, the womb from which all our thought and action are born. So, any issue can be understood only when the whole picture is perceived—not only its superficial but also its hidden aspects; and this totality naturally includes the relationship of the problem to man, the problem maker. Regardless of what psychoanalysts tell us, no part of the psyche can be completely understood without taking into account the whole field of the psyche. To examine this vast area, our usual piecemeal, analytical approach is to no avail. To discover something in its totality, in a flash, without the lengthy summation of a multitude of fragmentary bits of information, is the beginning of meditation.

3

Our
Predicament

It is sometimes said that man is his own worst enemy. This statement is particularly meaningful to the religiously minded person, that is, he who wants to investigate the nature of suffering and *what it is* that suffers.

That faculty of man that enables him to construct words and symbols apart from the things themselves—the discursive intellect—came about in the evolution of consciousness through the development of Memory. It has given man a great advantage over the other animals in the struggle for physical survival. It is this "analytical mind" that has played such an important role in the satisfying of his needs for food, clothing, shelter, transport, communications, and so forth, culminating in the marvels of modern science and technology.

This same specialization has, however, also had an un-favorable consequence in that it gave rise to an entire new world: the world of the imagination, which controls the greater part of man's conscious—and to an even larger extent, his unconscious—activities. Thus, man has become an animal that "suffers" through its own specialization. (If we look at biological evolution, we can find many examples of species that undermined their own existence and died out through overspecialization in one form or another.)

It is in this imagination that man sees himself as a separate psychological entity that needs to struggle to maintain its separateness, for its destruction, the extinction of the "I," is felt as death. Hence, as soon as the imagination has conjured up that bundle of desires and inclinations that has only one end—namely, to protect and expand this vulnerable self, which is threatened by the outside world (the nonself)—there is immediately fear. Thus, as long as there is any form of duality there is fear, insecurity, and the bondage of desire; all these go to produce suffering.

The remedy, of course, lies in reuniting the part with the whole; and this can take place only when it is clearly seen that the "part," the idea of the separate ego—produced by the imagination—was an illusion, a fraud, the result of Ignorance (cf. the first words of the Buddha after his enlightenment experience: "Desire, I know thy root, from imagination art thou born; no more shall I indulge in imagination, I shall have no desire any more.").

For, paradoxically, the bundle of desires that strives to build permanency and security for the ego *is* at once the ego. To put it slightly differently: Consciousness manifests itself in human behavior *as though* there were a permanent entity, an unchanging self, in each one of us.

To follow the various movements of the mind sponta-

14

neously—that is, without being driven by any compulsion, any motive—there must be the pure flame of interest. One might say that this condition of disinterested interest is the *sine qua non* for any effective approach to the spiritual life. This special kind of interest is really the beginning of love— a love of the problem, for its own sake. It cannot be cultivated, for then again the mind is in its usual state of end-gaining; and a love of something is always beyond any causation; it is its own justification.

So meditation is a process of "pure perception"—that is, without the slightest identification with what is perceived, and so without wish to change it. We simply look at the mind's agitation and refuse to be dragged down the drain of "individuality," though this refusal is not an act of will but becomes a fact spontaneously in this state of Total or Bare Attention when the mind is no longer ensnared in any of the many ways by which it can deceive itself. It is important to see that Bare Attention (in which there is no longer an entity that is attentive) is something utterly different from "introspection," which is a form of self-analysis in which there is the analyst and the analyzed (the analyst not realizing that he is also part of the analyzed).

When the mind is in this unique state in which "perception" is no longer split into the percipient and his perception, then there is a momentary elimination of the imagination and a flash of clarity. This happens because the self, in that single moment, is no longer strengthened at the center, and its elements, being "recognized," just fall apart.

These moments of clarity enable us to see how our psychological activities are bound to "time," in that each belongs to some habitual pattern of behavior. The "seeing" of the chain of cause-and-effects of desire acting itself out in the present moment has an immediate liberating effect, for then we realize that no desire stands on its own, that none has an absolute reality, but that all desire is merely a reaction to a previous conditioning influence. This is the realization of the Void, the emptiness of the whole world of thought and desire. Thus, by the process of meditation, a purification of the contents of our consciousness is set in motion. This is not however a process that takes place in time; it happens in flashes, from moment to moment. Krishnamurti once said that in one second of awareness the whole universe can be perceived.

To put the foregoing very simply: when Ignorance is exposed to Awareness, it is burned away and something entirely different comes into being. One could also say that once the meditator, the thinker, has understood himself completely, he ceases to be: the thinker and the thought have become one. However, to avoid misunderstanding and the deepening of existing confusion about our self-nature, one should hasten to add that basically there never has been any separation, and that the fundamental reality of their unity now becomes, in addition, *an empirical fact*. We cannot put Enlightenment in opposition to Ignorance; otherwise we create only another pair of opposites, and any pair of opposites consists of relativities that can be transcended. Nirvana comes about when all dualistic notions such as "good and bad," "happiness and suffering," "the one and the many," and the like, have been transcended. Or in less scholastic language, it comes with the emergence of "love" and the disappearance of all self-ish thought. In this state, action is cut free from thought for its fruits—and that is the only action in the world that does not lead to further misery and confusion.

16

4

On
Mindfulness*

Some time ago *The Hibbert Journal* published a report of a philosophers' conference in Hawaii.† One of the delegates at this meeting, a Professor Northrop, expressed the view that the present world situation was not simply a battle between communism and capitalism, or between East and West, but between enlightenment and darkness in the individual mind. This seems a remarkable statement to come from the mouth of a philosopher, and one which immediately directs attention to the area where *all* our

* A talk given to the London Buddhist Society and the Theosophical Society, Wimbledon Lodge, England.
† The Third East-West Philosophers' Conference, held in Honolulu, Hawaii, 1959.

problems originate, whether they be personal or collective; for, as Krishnamurti expressed it so well: "The world problem is the individual problem and the individual problem is the world problem."

Now you may wonder what all this has to do with mindfulness? I think it has a great deal to do with it, the crucial question being: On which side am I in the present worldwide crisis? For, although I may have the best intentions in the world in trying to be "good," not being mindful and therefore not clear in my mind, I am a prey to exploitation, and so, willy-nilly, strengthen the destructive forces.

Only through mindfulness can I obtain understanding of myself, or rather: mindfulness *is* understanding. In that state I can no longer be exploited. This is no mere "sales resistance" but signifies the complete absence of the "buyer" as a psychological entity, whether faced with superfluous material, political, or spiritual goods.

My having said all this, you will probably be impatient to hear from me how to be mindful, how to meditate. So I would like to make it clear from the outset that with regard to the mindfulness I am talking about, there is no "how." It is not something that can be simply practiced or cultivated. It comes into being spontaneously, once a right set of conditions is fulfilled. Therefore I cannot teach you or demonstrate how to do it. But what I am concerned with is to show you what mindfulness *is*.

Now if we can listen with the argumentative side of our minds temporarily in abeyance, then perhaps each one of us may find out for himself what it means to be mindful. Not to be argumentative implies to be in a state of not-knowing, for all of us, including the speaker; so let us go exploring through this uncharted land of the mind and regard it as an exciting adventure, because we do not know and do not care where it will lead us.

In order to see what mindfulness is, it might first be useful to see what it is not, and why there is no method that can help us toward its achievement. We know there are many so-called "ways" being advocated that all promise to lead us to the goal, and uncritically many people throw themselves at the mercy of some teacher, some Society or Church. Some of us have gone from Society to Society until we end up in this one, where we are promised nothing, but instead are told we shall have to work things out for ourselves if we desire to find salvation . . . When finally the moment has arrived and we feel the need to take stock of our search and of our present degree of understanding, it seems imperative to me that we reexamine our point of departure by asking a few fundamental questions: Is there a Way at all? A Way toward what?, and What is it that we are seeking?—questions we should really have asked at the very beginning of our search.

Even a superficial examination of the diverse methods purporting to lead to Liberation will reveal that not only do they all differ, but each one of them is suffering from an inherent contradiction. All teachers say that there is a path along which it is possible to approach the goal stage by stage. What they infer is that by the gradual acquisition of wisdom one's self can be perfected. (This notwithstanding, some of these teachers tell us, almost in the same breath, that Reality is nondual and that therefore there is no such thing as a "self.")

Now either there is an entity that can be enriched, perfected, or what have you, in which case I should continually busy myself in beautifying this entity in all respects, by training, discipline, and so forth; or there is no such thing at all, and I am merely enacting the ridiculous farce of keeping this illusory entity alive. So before I get completely bogged down in the morass of contradictory teachings, the first thing I shall have to find out is whether or not there is an enduring entity— for everything hinges on that.

This is what is called in Buddhism the problem of "anatta" (nonself). Now I would like to suggest that what is required is not to accept or reject anatta, but to come to an understanding of the mechanism of the mind. And I think there is a delightfully simple way to see the essential thing in this connection. Let us ask ourselves the pertinent question: "Is the thinker different from his thought?" Is there inside me a factory turning out an endless string of thought sausages? What happens when thought comes to an end (as, for instance, in dreamless sleep)? And is there then still a thinker? The answer to these questions can only be that never at any time is there an awareness of anything but thought. The notion of a separate thinker has arisen through memory and the incredible speed with which one thought follows another. This is somewhat similar to the mechanism of cine projection where dozens of individual frames of, say, a man's consecutive positions in walking appear on the screen as one continuous, integrated movement. But there it is not too difficult to understand that the whole thing is an optical illusion, due to the fact that the eye is too slow to isolate the separate frames flashed onto the screen with great speed the result being that the images flow into one another, giving the characteristic but false impression of continuity.

This new fact which we have just discovered, that of the discontinuity and so the unreality of the thinker, follows of course also from the easily observable fact of the transiency of all things: everything is continuously in a flux; hence there can be no enduring entities of any kind. Consequently, nothing has any self-nature or permanent identity.

Scientists, on the basis of their experience, have come to the conclusion: "Nature abhors a vacuum," and this has become a well-known dictum among them. Similarly, one might say: "Thought abhors a void." Because of this, thought gives itself continuity, permanency, and security, by means of memory. From this it creates a picture of an imaginary entity, the "I," the thinker. This is the first delusion from which all others follow. This "I" (which is thought identified with the idea of permanency) then tries to work upon thought, to ennoble and mold it after the ideal, causing contradiction and pain. But as little as a knife can cut itself, can thought be incisive with regard to itself. Yet this is what priests of various denominations have tried to achieve for centuries—needless to say, without the slightest success. The same observation applies to the failure of introspective analysis in effecting a transformation of the mind.

Perhaps we can now better understand the words of Zen Master Seng-tsan when he stated: "If you work on your mind with your mind, how can you avoid an immense confusion?" All this means then that the mind by its own efforts is incapable of setting itself free. Another famous Zen Master, Bankei, compared this vain effort at liberation with "washing off blood with blood."

The important question which must present itself at this stage of our inquiry is: "Can the unreal self be dissolved?" We all know that a piece of dangerous machinery, like an unexploded mine, can be dismantled quickly and efficiently only if we know accurately how it was originally assembled. Just so with the equally undesirable machinery of the "I"—the cause of all suffering—which is put together by time and in time: only when we can consciously put it together, can we take it apart and so do away with it.

The "I" comes into being through bodily sensation and perception. It is not the "I" which causes thought, perception, consciousness, but the reverse: all these go to create the "I." Once this entity is born it begins to grasp and cling, and through this, self-consciousness is created.

Further, the "I," once formed, not only wants to grasp, but desiring at the same time to be socially accepted, is forced to do so in a covert manner so that its intent is not too obvious. This situation gives rise to the basic neurotic conflict, that is, the division and antagonism between two parts of the mind: the lower ego that wants to have it all its own way, and the so-called better or higher ego (also called the censor, in psychoanalytical parlance), which desires respectability and generally wishes to conform to Society—at least in surface appearance. The environment in which we live creates a further complication: the prevailing psychological climate demands a certain degree of sophistication in social intercourse. This has led to the personality cult. It is important to have the "right" sort of personality to "get on" in the world, whatever that may mean. The word "personality" comes from the Latin "persona," signifying "mask"; so our masks are becoming ever more complicated, and what is worse, we are becoming ever more identified with our masks (which means that in the end we are no longer even aware of the fact that we are wearing masks). Not only is the power which Illusion holds over our minds thereby strengthened, but there is also a

growing strain that all our reactions should be "just right"—
and the moment our psychological feed-back system breaks
down, neurosis develops.

As a practical example of how our psychosomatic make-
up has gone astray, we may take the case of the secretion
of adrenalin, a natural process which takes place whenever
the organism faces physical danger. This substance shortens
the reaction time and therefore increases the survival value
of the individual (it operates what physiologists term the
"fight or flight mechanism"). Now what happens in our so-
called civilized man? He secretes adrenalin as an emotional
reaction every time he finds himself in a psychologically
hostile atmosphere, or to put it differently, whenever his
urge for self-assertion and expansion is frustrated. Not only
does this reaction serve no purpose whatever, but ac-
cumulatively it acts like a boomerang on the organism,
causing psychosomatic disease. This whole process is of
course subconscious, just because we have not recognized
the "I" for the trick which it is.

Being aware of all the activities of the "I," not abstractly,
but actually from moment to moment—this, to me, is true
meditation or mindfulness; and, it appears, there is absolutely nothing to take its place for knowing oneself. As I
mentioned earlier, it comes into being spontaneously if the
right conditions prevail.

We shall now examine what those conditions are. The
main requirement is that one is vitally interested without
having any motive whatsoever; this condition is rarely met,
for it entails that one really loves to go into a problem, to
resolve it regardless of where it may lead. Yet it is important
to perceive its necessity. The moment one has a motive,
there is the urge to gain, and once again one is caught in

the process of becoming, of creating an artificial entity that accumulates and thereby gives rise to the illusion of continuity.

The second condition is that one remains completely passive in one's observation without the wish to change anything one observes. The third is that one does not accumulate the experience which mindfulness brings, because then, for obvious reasons, one undoes all the good work again. This means that although we use the term "self-knowledge," there is really only "self-knowing," from moment to moment, in mindfulness—which is obviously an entirely different thing.

When looking at the trees, the flowers, the handiwork of nature around us, there is spontaneously this kind of attention, for then we are disinterestedly interested and do not condemn or justify the objects of our attention. For example, we do not criticize the tiger for its ferocity. Nor do we identify ourselves emotionally with the experience, so there is no storing up. Thus, it can be seen that all three conditions are indeed fulfilled in this case.

So we must now ask ourselves: Can I have an extensional awareness that comprises not only the natural phenomena outside my skin, but also those within, that is, the thoughts, emotions, and the many urges that agitate the mind? The difficulty here is that we are so rooted in our attitude of being VIP's to ourselves that we can no longer look at our own thoughts dispassionately, and so regard them too as natural phenomena. We have created a fixed point from which all our thinking proceeds: *I* want to be happy, so *I* must meditate; everything seems to revolve around that "I."

On the other hand, the moment I just observe, without

wanting to change anything, I become, as it were, an objective onlooker, for then I no longer have a vested interest in the results of any thought processes. So no longer is there a fixed point, but only thought following upon thought; the "I" is no longer important. In this condition it feels almost as though I am standing outside myself.

What happens in awareness, therefore, is that thought momentarily loses its self-centered and enslaving quality. Thought is the movement of the self and needs that self in order to exist; when the domination of the self ceases, thought loses its compulsive force, its time-binding propensity. This relaxation enables me to realize what I am, a focus of pyschological tensions. I have at that moment solved the problem of "anatta"; thought ends as desire and things are seen directly and in their totality. This happens when the thinker and the thought have become one. However, no verbal description can convey the meaning of true mindfulness; it is something that everyone has to experience for himself.

In conclusion I would like to say to those people who are perhaps a little disappointed that I have not told them anything more positive, that in the spiritual life negative thought is the highest form of thinking. The point is that we never ask ourselves whether the question "What can we do?" is a legitimate one. If Reality is nondual, because my separateness is seen to be an illusion, does not then any effort on my part, any movement toward salvation, set up duality? Try what I may, I do not think I can escape from this dilemma.

To say we can do nothing is not Quietism, for Quietism is actually Sleep. Mindfulness, on the other hand, to give complete attention without judgment, without wanting any results from it, requires the fullest alertness—it really is a kind of mental Judo; and there is no end to it.

The two fundamentally different approaches to the problem of salvation seem to me well illustrated by an episode in the New Testament, as represented by the different attitudes of Martha and Mary. Christ comes to a village and a woman called Martha welcomes him to her house. Martha makes a great show of her solicitude for the Master and she seems to symbolize the way of action. Her sister Mary, on the other hand, sits quietly at his feet, listening in rapt attention. Martha chides her sister for not helping her. But Christ has this to say to her: "Martha, my dear, you are worried and bothered about providing so many things; but only a few things are really needed, perhaps only one. Mary has chosen the better part and you must not tear it away from her."

To perceive directly the necessity for this "one thing," this negative thinking, and *why* we can do nothing, that in itself is the beginning of true meditation. That insight will produce its own action without our having to do anything about it; Reality starts operating upon us instead of us operating on Reality.

True awareness begins with the realization that we are not aware, that our minds are distracted, that we compare, make moral judgments based on our particular conditioning —in short, that we always look at the world through the spectacles of the "I." It begins with the observation that all our strivings, all our cerebral and emotional activities, are but the movements of the self toward or from something, caught as we are within the opposites.

Therefore, the person who is really serious about these things will not leave this meeting with his mind occupied with such questions as "What can I do?," "What is the right way to meditate?," "Who is the right Master?," but with his attention turned inward, anxious to explore his mind, knowing now at least what the central issue is. Once this has become a fact, he will have discovered where the real treasure lies; he will need no teacher, nor will he need to read a single book or attend another lecture, for then he will be a light unto himself.

5

Living
in
the
Essential

(The correspondence scattered throughout these pages represents a fair selection of actual letters, believed to be of wider interest, received and answered by the author over a number of years. Expressing a variety of viewpoints, its inclusion was considered to make the book more of a public forum and correspondingly less of an author's dissertation. In this way, it is hoped, the work may contribute more effectively towards a much needed discussion of fundamental and urgent issues based upon independent inquiry rather than on a mere acceptance of someone's thoughts and opinions.)

Mrs. J.S., Johannesburg, South Africa

Dear Mr. Powell,

   I wonder if this letter will ever reach you. Have just

finished your book *Zen and Reality.** So many things have been clarified, and your remarks and extracts from Krishnamurti have been made especially interesting as I have studied him for a number of years. How interesting and absorbing this subject is; it seems to be the only thing that matters, after seeing the futility of everything. I went through a period of great melancholy and self-pity, and felt that Life was playing some horrible trick on humanity, but now I see that all conflict was created by myself—the self, the taker-away of all happiness.

Krishnamurti's remarks about the self feeding on self from moment to moment is indeed a grave and pertinent statement, and this has opened the door; now one can see the importance of this "moment-to-moment" watching the movement of thought. It seems truly to end time.

All our wanting to know, to seek, seems but an illusion, and all we need is to listen. How wonderful to get rid of all the rubbish that we prided ourselves on having learned, and live in a different kind of world, where nothing really matters anymore—and if it matters, why does it matter?

Very few people are interested in this very important subject, and it is a feeling of great elation to learn that there are some who have liberated themselves from the conflicts and sorrows of this world.

Sincerely,
J.S.

Dear Mrs. S.,

It is unfortunately true, as you write, that "very few people are interested in this very important subject"—and one may ask, of those who claim to take an interest, how

---

* Robert Powell, *Zen and Reality*, London, Geo. Allen & Unwin, 1961.

many do really understand what it is all about, and how many are really serious about these matters?

The momentous discovery that one's "self" is the cause of all misery—and paradoxically, that includes also one's own sorrow—means that for the first time one becomes wholly responsible. When one realizes that it is one's thoughts that cause the unhappiness—and not something external—then there is the right foundation, the right starting point, for meditation; never again will one look up to any Authority, to anything beyond one's own control, for guidance, salvation.

But also, it follows that when we say, as you do in your letter, "nothing really matters anymore," this is true only up to a point. For, paradoxically, it may be equally valid to state that when there has been this essential insight into the inherent emptiness of all things, it matters greatly what we do, think, and say. More than ever does it then matter whether we live in the Essential (which one might perhaps equate with the "spiritual life"—a life devoid of all superfluity), or whether due to our inertia we fall back into our old "selves," living in conflict and creating around us more confusion, more conflict.

All this requires energy, to see from moment to moment without depending upon the movement of time—which is choiceless awareness. One of the greatest illusions is to think that once we have acquired a general theoretical understanding of the ways of thought, we can relax—then we have "arrived." To me, there is no arriving at all, only traveling—an endless journey!

Many books have been written—and perhaps *Zen and Reality* has been guilty of this, too—which tend to create the impression that there is a once-and-for-all state, like an examination passed, after which the mind can afford to rest on its laurels. Again, this kind of assumption is based on a false idea of Continuity. For, as you write, when there is Awareness, when one lives with facts, with Reality, there is absolutely no continuity—time has come to an end. However, the moment we cease being aware, there is again the old duality of the observer and the observed: the observer with all his memories and all his experiences, opinions, looking from that background at the "observed," and so inevitably missing the fact. So each moment may be a fresh discovery, and Life a never ending process of learning.

Sincerely,
R.P.

6

A Noncomparative Look
at
Zen
and
Krishnamurti

One often hears the question being asked, "What is the difference, if any, between the teachings of Zen Buddhism and Krishnamurti?" and because of its implications to the leading of a truly religious life, it may perhaps be worthwhile to go into the matter.

As far as the present writer is concerned, there is neither Zen Buddhism nor Krishnamurti as a spiritual authority or a "teaching." Having understood the whole nature of authority and doctrine, these are immediately put aside, as having no meaning and no relevance to the way of life that ever proceeds from fact to fact. The truth of what *is*, is ever changing with time; it cannot therefore be "passed on," formulated, or its "attainment" made into a goal; there is nothing to be taught. That truth can only be discovered by the individual who is totally alert and completely free from any influence, any authority. For such a mind to be a "follower" of Zen, or of Krishnamurti—or anyone else for that matter—is entirely unthinkable.

All that the organized religions have done so far is to propagate an idea—whether it be God, Nirvana, or something else is immaterial—and to make everything subservient to that concept. And when every fact is immediately interpreted in terms of an idea, there can be no proper perception, no understanding of the real world. Facts then cease to have any significance, and we live entirely by and for the idea. All this is only too obvious when we look around us and see men everywhere the slaves of so many ideas: Roman Catholicism, Communism, Nonviolence, Black Power, and so forth.

If therefore Zen and Krishnamurti have any significance at all, their value must lie exactly in this negative aspect, of *not* offering men what they are so accustomed to look for—a set of ideas—and of denying us the slightest scrap of comfort. If, in addition, they force us to look within, even if it means being driven into a corner so that we *must* face even the most unpleasant facts about ourselves and recognize that we blindly adhere to an *idea* about ourselves—that we are divine, immortal, sons of God, or any of the other nonsense in which we believe—then they can help us toward a right beginning to a religious life.

So let us first have a look at Zen Buddhism. One thing that follows immediately from what we have stated above is that there can be no Zen Buddhism as an "ism." There is only the individual who understands himself and in the light of that understanding makes an "enlightened" statement—you may call him "liberated" or a Zen Master, if you like, but why label him?—and if that is so, then paradoxically there is no Zen at all! An intimation (which is a hint, not a "teaching") of the Truth can only be given by a man who is in a state of creativity, which implies uniqueness. All else is mere imitation, repetition of someone else's discovery and has therefore lost all vitality. To state something original, it must be realized at that moment by the speaker or writer; otherwise to him it is not true, it has no validity. Although there is only one Truth, this may be expressed in a million different ways; and such an expression has no utilitarian value, it is not something that can be learned by rote and applied in daily life, as the organized religions would have us do.

Having come thus far, it already becomes clear that the question starting off this chapter is not the right question to ask at all; and we have seen elsewhere that a wrong question can never produce the right answer. The question implied a comparative examination, and a comparison can be applied only to definite teachings, doctrines. But in the absence of those, where we are dealing only with individuals who refuse to serve as our guides but tell us to stand on our own feet, what is there to compare? Is it not like trying to grasp the wind within our fist?

Our examination of Zen and Krishnamurti must therefore be on a strictly noncomparative basis, for as soon as we start to compare we are lost, comparison, evaluation, entailing judgment, which in turn depends on conditioning; thus, comparison can in no way lead to a fundamental understanding of anything.

Perhaps the right question would have been: "To a person wishing to lead a spiritual life, which teaching is going to prove the truly helpful one—Krishnamurti's or that of a particular individual whose name is associated with Zen?" To which the answer must be: "That depends entirely on what is said and not on who says it." In other words, "anything may be of help and anything may be a hindrance," but if we know how to listen, even the false may be seen to have significance and could lead to the discovery of what is true.

It will be appreciated that any positive statement about the Unknown, anything that posits a certainty and gives us "hope," must be a hindrance—for the mind, being what it is, will immediately elevate this "description" to a goal and thereby effectively block any real discovery. With this understanding, let us examine what Professor D. T. Suzuki said during a talk at the London Buddhist Society on "Faith in Zen Buddhism."* In this lecture he stated: ". . . there is something which one has to develop from within oneself, and this something which develops becomes conscious within oneself. This is Zen faith." Yes, of course, one can start only with oneself, and when the machinations of that petty self are observed, it is obvious that something else (which we do not know and cannot know, when all thought, all activity, at present lies within a circle of the self's limitation) must take its place.

But then, what do we make of the following remarks about the "self": "Now look within yourself and see how rich you are. You have nothing to lose, you have nothing to gain. Everything you need is there, but you are generally not conscious of the fact that you are immensely rich. The inner self or soul or mind is filled with everything that you

* June 19, 1958 (as reported in the August 1967 issue of *The Middle Way*).

need; there is nothing else to be looked for. While we are not conscious of this we look for that treasure, but the fact that we seek the treasure somewhere outside proves that it is in everyone of us. If the treasure were not in me already, I would never think of gaining it. The very reason that makes me look for the treasure, even outside, shows that I must have seen the treasure somewhere. The treasure must be in me otherwise I would have no thought of seeking it."

Notwithstanding the great emphasis laid by Professor Suzuki on this point, is his conclusion logically correct? (For example, men have always sought to construct a perpetual motion machine, but does that prove its feasibility?) Is it even in accordance with reality to state that the treasure lies within me? It is here that a certain amount of doubt seems justified. (The Kingdom of Heaven may well be within, but first it has to be discovered; until its discovery by the individual it is, to all practical purposes, nonexistent.) Does Professor Suzuki's description of the self indicate what we really are, or does it reflect a concept, an idea about the self?

The underlying question seems to be: Is there a part in me that is not conditioned, beyond space and time, and therefore, "immortal"?

All the organized religions (with the exception of Buddhism) have conditioned us to accept, to believe, that there is something divine, something eternal in us: the "soul," the "Atman," and so forth. But if we really look without the burden of tradition, does it not become clear that the mind is totally conditioned, totally ego-centered; that our nobler aspirations are the mere projections from an ego that knows no inward richness, and that these aspirations are therefore still colored by that poverty? Is not the opposite contained within itself? That we are seeking something is obvious, but do we know what we are seeking?

It seems to me that what we are searching for is only a way out of our misery and boredom: the Utopia is self-projected. This projection is also a very convenient device for the ego, since it admits of Time. If we are partly pure, then it is a matter of mere adjustment, which can be gradual, and therefore constitutes an endless postponement and not a radical revolution, not an immediate cutting away of greed, violence, self-interest, of which the ego is composed.

In the next paragraph of the article cited, Professor Suzuki states along analogous lines that we seek immortality because there is something immortal in everyone of us, but we are not conscious of that fact: "When Buddhists deny the existence of an ego or ego-substance, or when they talk about the transiency of things, this is not an expression of negativity. Underneath, behind the apparent negative statement, there is a grand, basic primary affirmation." And later: ". . . the absolute self might be termed other, Absolutely Not-self. For if the self is called Absolute Subject or absolute subjectivity, then the absolute subjectivity is identical with Absolute Objectivity."

I feel it is fair comment to state that these words, even though possibly meaningful at a certain level of comprehension, hold but little or no meaning to a suffering, confused ego. What is immediately meaningful and valuable only to that entity is to face honestly and squarely the conflicts and problems by which it is beset. Anything else is likely to throw us off the track.

Although Zen is claimed by Suzuki and others to be strictly nonintellectual, in this sample one of its foremost

37

expounders appears to cater directly to the Western taste for the metaphysical, with its addiction to ideas and concepts.

What about Krishnamurti? Throughout all his recorded talks and writings there are no conclusions, nothing is posited or taken for granted, and no solution to any particular problem is indicated. There is absolutely nothing for the mind to build on, no certainty of any kind to give it hope or serve as a moral crutch.

The patient is very ill, and what good does it do him to be lectured on the ultimate state, the condition which will prevail after a cure has been effected? To feed him with concepts and theories, will this make him strong again? Most of the time the patient is not even aware of his own serious condition; and Krishnamurti forces him, as it were, to discover it for himself, to look at every aspect of the illness, for only in understanding his essential ill functioning lies the remedy, leading to its cessation.

Krishnamurti is not a mind doctor, who administers some prescription, some formula for healthy living, or a tranquilizer to quiet the patient. He leaves it entirely to the patient to cure himself, since only in the total understanding of one's own unhealthy, psychological tendencies lies the possibility of a healthy functioning. Therefore, he has no "disciples" or "followers," and those who describe themselves as such (if there be any), or who give others this label, have not yet understood a thing.

7

The
Problem
of
Ambition

L.M., St. Albans, Herts.

Dear Mr. Powell,

I have read your article, "Despair, Emptiness and Otherness," in *The Middle Way* several times. I am very sensitive to what you have written. You seem to "speak to my condition," as the Quakers say.

"Most of us are engaged in the pursuit of some goal . . ." Yes, up to the age of fifty I kept myself in a state of excitement, mild or intense, with the thought of reaching a goal. This, to me, was life. And then I realized that my ambitions would never be achieved. I was a failure. Despair and Emptiness were mine.

Frequently I am plunged into the depths on meeting with a little disappointment. I know it is unreasonable to

39

feel badly because I have failed to achieve a desire. Even writing this down, makes me see again how stupid it all is.

A few years ago I took up oil painting as a hobby to fill the gap a little. I now understand I paint to please myself and to get praise from others. As I have progressed in this, so I have progressed in understanding the truth of my real motives and I realize the painting is of little consequence. And for that matter, so am I.

I am afraid the last paragraph of your article beats me. I will enclose a stamp in the hope that you might find time for a reply.

Thanks for your article.

Your sincerely,
L.M.

Dear Mr. M.,

To be invited to comment upon the issues raised in your letter of October 17, leaves me with a feeling of helplessness—for more than one reason. In the first place, no problem can be dealt with adequately in isolation, on its own level, although we are accustomed to doing just that, and therefore ever create fresh problems. What needs to be tackled is the soil in which problems take root, so that one can cope immediately with any and every problem—and this involves a revolution in one's whole outlook on life. Secondly, such a transformation and the ferment in the mind which must necessarily precede it are essentially private and intimate matters. It requires hard work of a very special kind.

To read, to correspond, to talk *about* these things is largely irrelevant. It is like learning the basic strokes of swimming on land, without ever touching the water. To understand this one point only, that I feel is as much as one may ever expect from any discourse; and this could well be the only right beginning, in which one finds oneself suddenly and easily "in the swim."

First and foremost, it must be understood that psychological problems, unlike material, technical problems, are not imposed on us from the outside world. If they were, they would be relatively easy to solve: sooner or later, by the application of the relevant knowledge, a method or a technique, the correct solution would be discovered.

With any psychological problem, however, what is at fault is an inherent malfunctioning of the mind itself—in other words, the problem is of the mind's own making. Thus, although we are wont to express the problem in terms of external circumstances, these are in reality quite irrelevant. Therefore, although man is his own worst enemy, he is also—and just because of that—his own liberator.

The necessary revolution in the functioning of the mind cannot, however, be brought about without having a certain amount of insight into what one *is*. This implies sensitivity to one's present state of malfunctioning—without as yet coming forward with any remedies—and the observation of how one's mental processes are full of contradiction and so continually give rise to conflict. Is it at all likely therefore that this mutation in the mind can be brought about merely by attending classes, discussing philosophies, and so forth, with other people who may be equally confused?

Unfortunately, I feel, the new consciousness is not so easily come by. Its advent requires a great deal of perseverance, patience, and the ability and readiness to think things through to the very end, regardless of consequences. And most of us are content to treat the symptoms rather than the disease. The problem of despair, the pain of frustration, of not having succeeded in life, although one may have lived for half a century or more and contantly struggled to achieve all sorts of things, remains unsolved. Temporarily it can be pushed into the background when the conscious mind engages in some activity for the sake of activity—perhaps in a hobby, or any of the other innumerable escapes which we have—but beneath it all remains the gnawing feeling of emptiness, misery. And when on rare occasions we do take stock and see the utter emptiness and futility of our lives, there is mere resignation, helplessness, but still no breakthrough.

Dear Mr. M., please understand, this is not just *your* difficulty; it has become a tremendous problem with almost everyone, because the way we live is so completely mechanical and we are so little conscious of what is driving us.

Only the mind that has the capacity to perceive its own contradictions and illusions can free itself. After all, what is a problem? How does conflict arise? Does not conflict arise when the mind is caught up in two or more incompatible desires? For example, I am told that ambition is unspiritual, destructive, and so forth, so I want to be rid of it. But basically I am still in its grip, because my desire to be free still forms part of ambition, is only another aspect of it. So now not only have I the problem of ambition, with all its accompanying frustration, but I have also created a second problem: how to get rid of it; and the more I struggle to be free, the greater is the clash of my desires, the more I find myself in bondage.

The truly free mind, on the other hand, is totally unconcerned with this whole issue of success or failure, not because it realizes its ambitions can never be achieved, but

42

because it understands there is nothing to achieve—or to put it slightly differently, there is nobody who achieves. Such a mind perceives that the urge to achieve, to be a so-called success, is only a social habit, or perhaps one should say, a social disease—but tremendously infectious.

It is therefore plainly not sufficient to say to oneself: "It is so silly to be ambitious, I mustn't"; one has to go into this whole question of desire and, more generally, of thought, and find out whether there is such a thing as individual thought at all, or whether perhaps all thought is part of the collective consciousness, a result of social conditioning.

And I feel very strongly that without understanding what one is integrally—which involves the question of one's identity—one can never be free, however much one may practice introspection, mind training, concentration, or meditation. When I say I must do this or that, who is this I? Has not the I come about through resistance, through conflict, and does it not epitomize the essence of ambition itself? Is not the I constantly being kept alive by experience, by building upon the accretions of Memory, and by making these experiences, these relationships with things and events gone by, into a frame of reference for all further action? This eternal burden of the past, which includes not only the knowledge and experience acquired in a lifetime but also the far-away past in the form of racial memory, constantly guides us in a certain direction and molds all thought and action into particular patterns. Thus there can never be a renewal, for all our actions are in some way dependent upon the past, and are therefore merely re-actions.

To unravel this very subtle machinery of the mind requires the utmost watchfulness; but once this is clearly perceived, is there then still this terribly binding obligation to the past, and is the past then still important? Pursuing this investigation to the very end, one may arrive at the discovery that this self-imposed tyranny of Memory finds no real basis but in our own thoughtlessness and lack of understanding of the ways of the mind. Seeing clearly that only the present exists, and that the past is what we choose to carry with us as memory but is actually completely finished, done with, we see a possibility of shaking off the yoke. For then it becomes apparent that to the extent to which I choose to live within and for an "identity," I invite sorrow and misery; but to the extent to which I discard this identity, because I see its emptiness and how it results from my mechanical way of living, I can jump out of my old skin, as it were, and open myself to a Happiness which is unconditional and unconditioned.

Once one has come thus far, but no sooner, it may be possible to stumble upon that state of Emptiness, in which there is no more conflict, no further despair, and in which all seeking and all travail have come to an end.

Sincerely,
R.P.

8

Only the Empty Mind
is Capable
of
True Thoughtfulness

Man, both individually and collectively, is the sum total of all that he has ever thought, experienced, known. His thought is the end product of a particular background, a certain mode of living, the culture in which he has been raised, and of various other factors that have molded his mind, such as climate and even the food he eats.

Therefore, we may state that man's thought expresses the essence of his being. The question whether he is anything besides his thought does not really arise at this point, because the way man functions at present he is entirely dominated by the processes of his mind—all his actions, feelings, and emotions are the result of cerebration.

Thought, except on the level of scientific thought, is always subjective. There is no such thing as objective thought; thought is always wide of the mark. Why? Because all thought is based on an illusion, on the idea that man as an individual has some absolute existence, represents a permanency in a world that is ever in total flux. We have taken for granted Descartes' famous dictum, "I think, therefore I am," without as much as a second thought.

The exact role that thought plays in the world of the scientist is not really relevant to this discussion; suffice it to say that thought can perform a useful function in that sphere only so long as it is not expected to furnish any ultimate answers, so long as it deals with correlating and quantifying relativities and one does not expect any "final solutions" to its equations. In this connection, the space-time framework that thought has erected is merely an aid in this process of science.

But on the psychological level, when we demand "understanding," that is, absolute insights and not mere correlations, thought is to be utterly distrusted because no psychological problem can ever be solved by thought activity. Is not this our real problem—perhaps the *only* one: our failure to realize that the pressures which have created our problems are the very same pressures that have molded the mind with which we try to solve the problems?

A space-time framework has been set up by our desires, based on psychological time—which is the urge to change what *is* into what *should be*—and in this great snare the mind has become entangled. This space-time framework is not something extraneous to man; he is the creator of it, although he acts as if it had an independent existence and he must continually oblige its demands.

Let us put this slightly differently. Thought, once arisen, is driven along by its own momentum, giving continuity to man as a psychological entity. Therefore, Thought *is*

Time; it is the tool, the medium, through which the mind strives for security; that is, it is ever engaged in securing its own gratification, establishing its comparative importance—all that being based on pleasure. Because this activity entails a goal, a fulfillment, something to live for, all its activities bring into being the future, that is, Time.

There is a strange paradox here. Man engages in thought because he believes he is something other than his thought —something more substantial and less transient. In other words, he has created a center from which all his thinking proceeds. This center then tries continually to manipulate thought for its own ends, making thought a worthless thing and a waste of energy.

It is because of this duality—of thought and the center —that Man lives in conflict. For, if I merely live my thoughts, I have peace. The center, however, acts like a censor, acting upon every experience, building upon every thought that arises, and in doing so generates further thought. The center must ever undergo fresh experience, new and continued pleasure, avoid pain, and so forth, and so the thinker is always active; the center is never at rest.

Now, what would happen if one could live with one's thoughts—without need for "second thoughts"—recognize them for what they are and not relate every thought to the center? And if one would observe, without saying of every observation: This is good, I must have more; that is bad, I must avoid . . .? Then, one would soon find that the center of recognition which is behind the driving and directing force of Desire, based on the pleasure/pain principle, is no longer fed and kept alive by our thoughts and experiences— and without the center, thought cannot long survive on its own.

When the compulsion to bring forth thought based on

self-interest (that is, the interests of the center) has collapsed, a rare quality comes into being, which we may perhaps designate as "true thoughtfulness." Language can be very misleading, and this particular term is a case in point. Real thoughtfulness, the capacity to be considerate, to be watchful of everything that goes on both outside and inside one's skin, with understanding, requires a mind that is alert, active—that responds to every challenge with the speed of lightning. Such a mind cannot be cluttered up with thought, with memory images, with unfulfilled desires; it is empty. It *has to* be empty, to be attentive, to be capable of action that is not a reaction, capable of seeing something totally.

Normally, our seeing is fragmentary, consisting in fitting an observation—or rather, the memory of it—into a pattern of memory images. It is like building up a photo album of the world, which we call "my experience," and which is the essence of the "me." Such seeing can only be lifeless, because it misses the whole vital dimension of the present; and the observation is always fragmentary, because it is totally involved with that "me."

True thoughtfulness, on the other hand, comes with the emptying of the mind. The empty mind is, paradoxically, an entirely different state from "thoughtlessness." Thoughtlessness is to be incapable of thought when such thought is appropriate and required; it is to be inaccurate in one's thought and observation; it is to be ignorant of the mechanism of thought; it is to be lacking in the understanding of one's relationships. Thoughtlessness is the inevitable result, the symptom, of the disease of being forever filled with thought, ideas.

Only an empty mind is capable of relationship; and it is

48

the only truly effective mind, because it can meet events, ideas, persons, with *complete* attention, in an act of total perception.

It is strange to consider that the knowledgeable mind has really very little scope in life. The mind that is burdened with the past, in the form of knowledge, experience, has usefulness on a certain level. It is obviously essential in the strictly limited area of scientific thought and in the business of making a livelihood, although even there, it is rapidly being overtaken by the computer and by mechanical documentation and information-retrieval systems. But in the much larger sphere of living, of coping with basic human problems, the knowledgeable mind seems to me the most overrated thing in the whole world. The empty mind is an innocent mind; and only with an innocent mind is there an end to thought and the problems which it engenders.

9

What Education Should Be
All About,
and What
it Actually is

Sadly, the above-named categories are two entirely different things. Should not education be concerned with pre-
paring us for living? After all, we have not always been in
this world, although the reincarnationists undoubtedly will
take exception to this statement. Therefore, as upon enter-
ing any arena, we badly need preparation. This is so especially in this case, since nobody ever asked to be born
into this absurd world, but we were—quite against our will
—literally and figuratively pushed into it.

What, actually, is education at present? It is no more than
the preparation for some job, and even at that often half-
hearted; and some lessons at gamesmanship so that we
may play our assigned social roles. In all, it amounts to no
more than an effort to fit the individual into the framework

of a miserable society, an effort in which it fortunately not always succeeds. Thus, the general mass of mediocrity which it turns out through its mills of gray uniformity is leavened with a handful of "misfits," "dissenters," "drop-outs from society"—call them whatever you like—which are the only hope of this world.

The general inappropriateness of our educational system is based on a number of misconceptions. One of the most important of these seems to me to be the entirely misplaced emphasis on the training of the intellect and the cultivation of memory—two kinds of human "capacity" which have their place in life, but are not of paramount importance to the individual. But people set undue store by them, because they believe it helps them to survive in a competitive society.

Oddly, what has value in living a full life—and we use "full" not in the sense of merely "experience-filled"—appears to have very little survival value in the present kind of world. On the other hand, it seems to me that an individual who is truly educated would be spared some of the harrowing experiences which many young people inevitably have to go through. Just at an age when sensitivity is at its highest, and not yet corrupted or deadened by the process of civilization, our youth are being exposed to a cruel and irrational world—without as much as a word of initiation from their peers. And in this connection, we are not just thinking of those children who come from so-called broken homes; even when "loved" by their parents the children are no better prepared to face life. This is simply because the parents do not have the necessary insights: they need first to be reeducated themselves. Or maybe, in spite of their protestations, they do not really love their children; otherwise they would make it their business to find out what the child really needs, and as a consequence we would have quite a different world. Is it not paradoxical that of all the animals the human species weans its young for the longest period of time, yet leaves them worst prepared to fend for themselves?

As we have already implied, it really comes down to a sense of values. Either we bring up individuals who will be first and foremost human beings, who can still savor the ecstasy of being alive as their natural birthright; or we go on turning out mechanical entities who have lost every form of sensitivity, who are so specialized—functionally—and therefore "restricted" that they hardly deserve the designation "human" but are really only poor imitations of our much-worshiped computer. If we opt for the latter, in our educational designs, then of course we shall continue to dehumanize and downgrade society. We shall end up with an increasingly grim world in which it will hardly be worthwhile, or even responsible, to bear and rear children. Perhaps this, then, will be the ultimate solution which our educational dilemma has in store for us.

Q   *What do you consider is going to be the main feature of Education of the New Man on the eve of the revolution in Consciousness? I mean, how are we to lay the right foundation for the emergence of the man in whom a revolution in consciousness has taken place?*

A   Ideally, the functions of Education in the new era of revolutionary consciousness—and I am not using this

* Certain questions and answers that came up during pertinent discussion meetings held by the author are reproduced here in the belief that they may be of wider interest.

term in any political sense—are threefold. First, education should be concerned with giving out the right information, correct facts, about the world in which we live and ourselves. At present, education purports to do just that, but its "facts" are not always correct. Paradoxically, although we live in the age of the so-called "information explosion," for most of us it is extremely difficult to get the correct information on anything that does not appertain to the physical sciences. Historically, sociologically, and economically facts are almost always colored, if not distorted. But could it be otherwise in a society where truth-for-its-own-sake is a coinage of little inherent value? It must be obvious that as long as people continue to be manipulated by powerful political, religious, and financial interests, the dividing line between truth and propaganda is likely to remain blurred. And so long as the teachers themselves are not independent from societal pressures exerted on them, it will be extremely difficult to convert the schools into oases of truthfulness in a desert of erroneous ideas and false values. And right now the schools themselves are shining beacons of conformity!

Then, there is the question of selectivity in the presentation of facts that has an important bearing on the dissemination of information. Obviously, to broadcast certain facts—even if 100 percent correct—but not *all* the relevant facts, is another way of distorting the truth. This is a well-established technique in the arsenal of those who wish to inflict their propaganda upon others. Yet, at the same time, there is a definite need for selectivity in using the vast quantity of material that we can teach our children. This is because, in some respects, the brain is a very inadequate computer; it can cope with only so much and no more, and we do not wish to burden the capacity for memory to any unnecessary extent. At present, the things we are learning in school are only too often found to have little practical and theoretical value in life. At the same time, a great number of facts essential to daily living are not taught at all or they are apparently not imparted with sufficient emphasis or clarity to take root. Let us take a simple example: masses of people still go through life without having the slightest idea of what constitutes a "balanced diet," or without any proper notions of their own physiology. What is needed, therefore, in the first place is a drastic revision of the curriculum, both as to fields of study and as to what constitutes the basics in each particular field.

Then, based upon the "right information" there can be "right thinking," and to foster this is obviously the second main function of education. It has been said many times before, but there seems no harm in repeating it here once again: In "right thinking" it is not *what* we think that is important, but *how* we think: the capacity to reason sanely and logically without being influenced in the least by emotion, by desire, by public opinion. Now it is possible to give someone a good grounding in logic—and this will be a necessary element in any teaching program—but beyond that nobody can really teach another person how to think. However, the teacher can do two important things to help: first, expose fallacious thinking wherever he sees it and however respectable the source; and secondly, never ram anything down a child's throat, but merely present him with the facts and let him get on with it. Then, there will never be any need to "isolate" the child from so-called "harmful influences" (if such a thing were possible at all) and thereby bring about a state of duality in which the child is ever vulnerable to succumb to those very same influences; but we give him the opportunity to establish a sense of values for himself that is based upon truth and not upon an artificial social morality. After all, what better basis is there for seeing one through life than being ever in close harmony with what *is*, even if it might get one into trouble with the traditional mores of the community?

Now with regard to the two main functions of education discussed so far, most secular schools will probably claim they are already well aware of the pertinent requirements; and that, however inadequately they are being met at present, they expect to make further significant progress in this direction. However, there is a third function of education about which nobody seems to be doing anything and which may well be the most important aspect of all. A child has a natural, inborn sense of wonder that in our present system is crushed at an early age. It is destroyed because the child is never left enough freedom to explore whatever is in the focus of his wonderment; he is never given enough time and opportunity to play, which, as may be easily observed, is one of the child's great learning avenues.* At the same time fear is inculcated through

---

* Readers of this book may be interested to know that educationalists have recently proved the value of just "messing about" in the learning process of young children. They found that when children in kindergarten are allowed a period of completely free play with their teaching materials

education being almost entirely achievement oriented. We are being educated in order to pass an exam, to hold down a job, and so forth. At every stage there looms the frightful prospect of failure, with all its attendant pain and suffering. Then through fear comes the urge to conform, to be safe at all costs, which is in direct contradiction to the aforementioned need for right thinking.

To help maintain some sanity in a society that is becoming increasingly more insane, it is imperative for the child not to lose contact with the source of his being, which contact is so abundantly present at an early age but through the pressures of civilization is becoming irretrievably lost.

One of the main reasons for this loss of sensitivity by the child toward everything around him is the fact that he is taught to function almost entirely cerebrally, which is a specialized way—because thought itself is essentially exclusive, specialized. So he is sucked into this mechanical process of collective thought before even having gathered a perspective on the scope, the purport, and the thrust of thought—and so loses his individuality. The child needs to discover for himself the limitations of thought; how all thought flows from self-orientation and therefore operates within a set frame of reference; how thought restricts and perverts every kind of perception, since even the simplest thought carries with it a whole world of implications, an entire heritage of presumptions and ideas about the

---

before being directed to work with them, they subsequently perform much better than when a much more "structural" beginning is imposed. ("Messing About in Science," by D. Hawkins and T. Kallet, in *Occasional Papers,* published by the Education Development Center, Newton, Mass.)

way things are and how they should be. Above all, and connected with this, the child needs to understand what is his "place in the world." By that phrase we do not mean the conventional dualistic concept which implies a separation between a "me" and the "world," but something quite to the contrary. We suggest that the child with his original purity of vision be left in peace with his innocent view of the world of which he is an integral part, having as yet little "self"-consciousness (which is really the feeling of separation).

Inherently, without any such notion as "his place in the world," the indoctrination that he must "become something" soon changes that. With the buildup of the many pressures from the collective, he soon adopts the artificial composite identity resulting from the various roles that society has assigned to him. And we all know how these roles have been arbitrarily assigned on the basis of parentage, inherited wealth, the so-called class" or caste into which one is born, and other such meaningless incidentals. The new education will be especially concerned with exposing the essential emptiness of all that conceptualization, this entire network of premises that supports the psychological structure of society, to the tremendous detriment of the individual.

So, when the child's vision remains pure, because he has seen through and rejected all the false thought structures that are pressed upon him and that pervert man's existence, he will not have any particular place in society—he will not belong anywhere, and therefore be at home everywhere. He will grow up as a man who is not rooted in any particular relationship or dependency; and because of that his action will ever be totally relevant, based only upon a perception of the facts and not upon any artificial ideological prejudices.

A person educated along those lines will also have a different attitude toward death. Because when one has no place in society, one has also no place *for* society. Therefore, not having staked one's happiness and integrity on it, there is nothing to lose nor to gain. One leaves the world as one entered it—*with* nothing and *as* nothing. Or, on a more fundamental level, as perhaps some Zen Master would phrase it: "the world (i.e., what *is*) is eternally there ("eternally" here being used in the timeless sense of "regardless of time"), and there is no one who enters it and no one who leaves it. Where then is cause for pain, for regrets?"

In all, we may perhaps best sum up the threefold task of education as the "preparation for dying as well as for living," of which paradoxically the former is the more important part. The preparation for living is basically concerned with physical survival and is of obvious value. However, when it is seen that the final act of physical death is a mere variant of the more general (psychological) dying, taking place at every moment of existence and forming an integral part of Life, then it will be appreciated that the education for death is not just to prepare for a particular moment in time, but it is to be concerned with the very essence of living.

Q *Are you not denigrating thought, which even the new man must be heavily involved with?*
A At present, man functions totally within the structure of thought, whatever his thinking or outlook may be.

Psychologically, emotionally, he is totally wrapped up with it; there is no part of him that is not subject to its dictates. He is totally "involved" and, therefore, the prisoner of thought. The new man, on the other hand, will be involved with thought only up to a point; and therefore he is not "involved" at all. His dealings with thought will be purely functional and momentary, and not psychological and protracted; for it is with him that the confusion between function and status ends. Thus, he will *use* thought rather than being manipulated, being molded, by it. From the vantage point of the old man, this way of life appears almost a kind of amphibian existence: there is still the same, if not greater, capacity to struggle with a problem technically and intellectually, to be apparently part of the going system, to fend for oneself in the rat race; but psychologically, deep down in the core of his being, this man remains untouched by the activity and so retains a lifeline to sanity. On that deeper level there is no struggle at all, because any such struggle emanates only from the urge to *be*, and the urge to be is the direct result of not yet having seen through the insignificance and emptiness of the self and its conceptual framework.

Because thinking, in the aspect with which we are here concerned, is ever I-oriented and therefore based on "being" at the exclusion of "nonbeing," no amount of thinking can come to terms with Life, which is at once being and nonbeing, birth and death. Individual consciousness is inherently preoccupied with psychological survival, and so thinking is the very birth of fear—the fear of Life as well as the fear of death that is part of it.

So, not only must the new education be devoid of the

insidious competitive element, because it is seen to be directly responsible for the assertion of being—or self-consciousness—in the child, but at the same time it must lead to a basic understanding of the very thinking process, so that there is a possibility of a quantum jump beyond both achievement and failure. Such education may impart something of real value: the capacity to function without fear, and therefore with dignity— a dignity that has absolutely no connection with status, as it is not yet debased by discriminatory thinking.

Q *Could you elaborate on your notion that education measurably contributes to our fear of death and that it is therefore also education that can help liberate man from this fear?*

A When the learning process is carried out within the context of a competitive system, it is always accompanied by the cultivation of fear. This is because competition implies reward and punishment, and in which the mere absence of reward in our social climate represents a special kind of punishment. True learning is possible only in an atmosphere of freedom, and this freedom is eroded by the pressure to succeed, which brings into being an entirely different factor: the urge to *be* and to assert that be-ing.

Learning is, among other things, the capacity to see things as they are, whereas fear always distorts that vision. Fear, like desire, is one of the most powerful causes of illusion: it makes man take a rope for a snake, and more generally, creates a whole world of fear-producing symbols out of "neutral" sense data. There is also the desire to change things in such a way

60

as to bring greater security; and the more we are active in this direction, the more we nurture the fear.

It can be seen how all this has a bearing on our attitude toward Death. If our educational system teaches that nothing succeeds like success, then this also means that nothing fails quite as abjectly as failure. To fail is a foretaste of death: it is "being cut down to size," whereas Death is the ultimate failure: being cut down to zero. So it is that education in its present form, with its strong emphasis on achievement as a preparation for living in a competitive society, is one of the major factors in inculcating the fear of death. True education, on the other hand, will be concerned with snapping out of this whole ignorant system of thinking. By letting the learning process blossom under its own impetus, it never encourages the urge toward being—or rather, toward *becoming* something other than what one is. Thus there is, as it were, a learning without a learner, since there is not the usual separation between the human being and the life that is him. Then, when there is no urge to *be* can there be fear?

Surely, the whole issue of death takes on a new perspective. When, in our everyday life, the perpetual struggle for all kinds of psychological ends ceases and there is peace, who is the entity that is still in this world and resists its own destruction?

I wonder how many of us have vitally experienced this thing we are talking about? Unless one is actually following this matter through to the end, these will remain meaningless words. And the difficulty is that, to do this, a great many things are involved—as one will find out soon enough if one tries it. One must divorce oneself from all rooted attitudes, from all forms of identification, from all relationships that have left a mark on the mind—in short: one must discard the many layers of what is called "personality," so painstakingly built up over a lifetime. One must give all that up, inconsequentially and without regrets, before one can be in the light. Then, once all the accretions of time are shed and one has disentangled oneself from the whole complicated and artificial structure of conventional, collective thought, it will be found that one is in this world, and yet one is not . . .; or, as it has been expressed: *in* this world, but not *of* it. In this extraordinary condition, which ordinary thinking will never fathom, one is living a kind of death, because then dying is part of living, and therefore there is no separation and so no fear.

Q   *Education as a preparation for death is not an entirely novel idea, as I understand it is found also in Japan; but to Western ears it sounds distressingly like a doctrine of Nihilism. Will such a negative outlook not lead to a general deterioration of standards and a lack of efficiency in all our enterprises? And will it not lead to frustration and despair when it is fully realized that personal glory from successful achievement does not amount to very much; that all our efforts will ultimately come to naught—in short, that there is really nothing worth living for?*

A   Quite to the contrary. When the essence of the structure of thought is understood, and it is seen how it engenders fear, then that very thinking apparatus becomes much more effective, much more penetrative, and is capable of going to the root of things. Then one can struggle with an issue, just for the hell of it—not because one *must* show a result for one's efforts or else be penalized; or because the conclusion from one's inquiry may answer some deep psychological need. In other words, the psychological struggles have made way for more purely intellectual and artistic exercises in which something is done out of love, and not because petty personal interests are involved with the outcome of the issue. In that there lies great joy, which is something quite different from the stimulating experience obtained from having scored a point. Such an attitude represents a virtual reversal of the existing order of things, in which nobody hardly ever does anything without "ulterior motives."

Anyway, is there not a general deterioration proceeding right now? And when posing the question were you not implying that anything done for gain or personal advancement is always done better than when it is done for its own sake? Our free-enterprise society likes to think it is so and propagates the idea, because it facilitates the exploitation of one individual by another. Our present educational system is subservient to this philosophy of the whip and the carrot; it is therefore quite content merely to prepare students for the corporations that are ever looking for human material that is "well motivated"—and so easily moldable by pressure, by fear. The new education, on the other hand, will be much more interested in turning out whole human beings for whom "work" and "job" have an entirely different significance.

Then, you ask, will the "negative outlook" not lead to

frustration and despair? Is there not great frustration and despair at this very moment? Can it be that education, as it is practiced now, is in itself a major cause of this frustration? As constituted at present, education is for the greater glory of something, whether of the self, the family, the race, or the nation, or whatever it may be. But the new education will help the individual to realize an infinitely greater glory that is ever there, in the present, available to everyone—whatever his antecedents, his knowledge, his qualifications—and need not, and in fact cannot, be struggled for as yet another achievement of man. Because we always look into the far distance, we do not notice what lies right at our feet. And although we cannot teach anyone how to find this glory, the mere fact of pointing out that such a thing exists, that there is a state of being in which one is completely part of all existence carrying with it a tremendous feeling of fulfillment, which is the true ecstasy, may help some youngster to find the treasure for himself.

10

If Awareness is Choiceless, Then Who is it That is Aware?

K. J. Bickley, Kent

Dear Mr. Powell,

For the third time I have just read your book "Zen and Reality" and have found it most helpful. I have also found a great puzzle in it! First, perhaps I should say that I *think* I understand the meaning of "not doing anything"—it seems to mean just living one's ordinary life, but with complete mindfulness. I hope this is correct. My stumbling block is found at the end of your chapter on Mindfulness where you say (page 50): "This mindfulness or awareness is not something that has to or can be practised; it comes to the awakened man spontaneously, in the same way that, say, beautiful music evokes a response in the sensitive listener." Now, I am neither an intellectual nor a very clever person, but this *seems* to say that "you must be aware (or mindful) in order to become enlightened but only the enlightened man is capable of being aware!" (On page 66 you suggest "awakening" as a more accurate word than "enlightenment"—or, in the above quotation from p. 50, are you using the word "awakened" as meaning—I quote from p. 67—"those who are interested in the Way and have an urge for Self-Realization"?) It's more than likely, of course, that somehow, somewhere I've misread what has preceded your chapter on Mindfulness, but I am unable to resolve this problem for myself and should welcome your help.

A further difficulty, of course, is the teaching that there is no entity. This gives rise to several questions whilst reading your book, *e.g.*:

p. 49, line 1   what "observes myself"?

p. 48, line 10   what "stops this process and reverses it"?

p. 22, line 22   what "is passively aware of the situation"?

p. 68, line 33   what "watches quietly with the greatest alertness"?

p. 29, line 16   what is it that is "mindful of every thought, every emotion, every image that comes to mind"?

I suppose all these questions are Zen koans! and equate with Ramana Maharshi's teaching of constantly asking oneself "Who am I?", "Who hears?", etc. More generally, how do you relate the latter's teaching to that of Krishnamurti and which do you suggest is the more valuable to the West?

I found your description of Buddhism as being a therapy intriguing and helpful, as well as being encouraged by your comment (on p. 68) that "the natural tendency (in life) is always for the greater to overcome the smaller." Please forgive me for encroaching on your time, but I should be grateful for your help.

Yours sincerely,

K. J.

Dear Mr. J.,

Thank you for your letter . . . I think I understand your difficulties, arising from the reading of "Zen and Reality." On page 50 I used the word "awakened" in the less ambitious sense of "alert," "sensitive" (corresponding roughly to its dictionary meaning), and not as a synonym of "enlightened," although on page 66 I suggested it might advantageously replace the latter term. Yes, indeed, one might equate such an "awakening" with a burning desire to undo the mental fetters which, after all, are of one's own making (indicated in different words on page 67). For this there must be attention to one's mental processes, and this attention is not the prerogative of the few who can say they have dispelled all traces of illusion from their minds and to whom we like to assign the label "enlightened," but it is possible for any of us willing to learn. To see clearly the activities of the self demands only a certain stillness of mind; where one cannot attain to this state in first instance, just observe the agitation of the mind, without getting caught up in it, and see if the mind does not settle by itself.

Regarding your other points, I feel the various questions raised by you boil down to this: "If awareness is choiceless, and therefore totally passive, then *who is it that is aware?*" It is the kind of question that is being asked again and again by students of Krishnamurti. Now first of all, in putting it, are we not begging the question? The grammatical

67

structure of the sentence implies that there must be a subject corresponding to the verb, in this case an entity who is aware. Because language reflects the usual patterns of our thinking, the implication is normally justified. But when it concerns fundamental questions, we cannot always be sure that the semantics are a reliable guide to comprehension. (It is not unlike the situation in modern physics, where the language of mathematics does not always yield insight into the real nature of fundamental particles or events.)

To go into this question more fully, let me take the example where the eyes are seing a mountain. I ask myself: "Is there an observer who is engaged in observing the mountain, or is there taking place an autonomous, natural process without duality, that is, without conscious effort on the part of the observer?" I maintain that if there is complete attention to the mountain, which means that one looks at it nongeologically, there is only that mountain and no observer whatsoever—which does *not* mean that the observer has become the mountain! The observer comes into being only when one starts looking at the mountain geologically, that is, with all one's knowledge and experience of mountains, saying: "What a lovely mountain!" or "It is frightfully barren," "It is a volcano," or anything of the sort.

Normally we look at anything analytically, with a specialized eye, from the background of our experience, and therefore in a fragmented way. The initial pure perception is immediately cut short by the analytical mind, which introduces a comparative, evaluative element in the observation and thus creates the "observer." Furthermore, perception is usually accompanied by either pain or pleasure; and the desire to perpetuate pleasure adds a new dimension to the observer; that is, it superimposes the psychological entity on the observer.

Thus, we might say that choiceless awareness, in which there is no entity that is aware, entails looking at an object without thought; in the above example it would mean to look at a mountain in the same way that one looks at a flat piece of ground. (Could this perhaps be the meaning of that old Chinese saying: "When I began to study Zen, mountains were mountains; when I thought I understood Zen, mountains were not mountains; but when I came to full knowledge of Zen, mountains were again mountains"?* If I can look in this way, and not only at a mountain but at a woman, a man, a child—in short, at everything around me —as well as at all that goes on psychologically within my skin, then I shall find that I no longer nurture a center of conditioning and so strengthen the subconscious.

For example, when I observe in myself greed, violence, sensuality, etc., the mind through recognition affixes the appropriate labels and sets thereby in motion the whole comparative, evaluative process of thought which has been conditioned by social morality to condemn or approve. Consequently, the mind might then endeavor to attain the ideal of nongreed, nonviolence, nonsensuality, little by little, on the assumption that if sufficient effort is made over a long enough period of time, eventually the mind will be "purified." Thus the psychological fact—that is, my actual condition—which is the Unknown because we never come in direct contact with it—is ever reduced to the known, a concept projected by thought. Now Krishnamurti maintains

* Attributed to Ch'ing Yuan, as quoted by Prof. D. T. Suzuki in "The Role of Nature in Zen Buddhism," *Studies in Zen,* Rider, London, 1957, p. 187.

that if we can look with complete attention, without naming, comparing, and so on—all of which constitutes the mind's habitual reaction—the Unknown will reveal its significance to us, and it will be possible to rise beyond both greed and nongreed, violence and nonviolence, etc., not in time but immediately. This is so, he states, because at no time has there been an observer who is greedy, violent, etc., but merely a psychological state which has only momentary existence. When we create duality with the "observer" who observes his condition, naming it "greed," "violence," and the like, we perpetuate that state by triggering off a tug of war between greed and nongreed, a play of the opposites that has no end. In other words, when we try to become virtuous in the traditional, moral sense by self-improvement, there is nothing in store for us but bondage. But when the self is transcended in the actual process of self-knowing, there is an immediate freedom which is not a reaction to the bondage.

From your letter it appears that you are acquainted with Ramana Maharshi's teaching. If so, you may remember that he views both the observer and the object as ultimately unreal; on waking both appear simultaneously, in somewhat similar manner to the (mutually dependent) origination of the "I" and the "world" in a dream. At first glance, this might seem contradictory to the mechanism described above and to Krishnamurti's contention that there *is* an observer—even though this entity can be dissolved in a state of awareness. On closer examination, however, it will be seen that Krishnamurti's and Maharshi's views about phenomenal existence come to much the same thing.

First of all, it must be recognized that the teachings appear to differ because they employ—or rather, imply—different definitions of the "observer" and the "object." To Maharshi, all "things" are only reflections of the one Reality and as such have no existence of their own. Thus the "observer" and the "object," in the intervals during which they manifest themselves, have only a shadow-like existence. Krishnamurti is primarily interested in the "observer" as a *psychological* entity; and when he speaks of the "observer" it is in this sense only, since his whole teaching is psychological. Maharshi, on the other hand, treats the observer as a total entity (psyche + soma), which he calls the ego; and he further deals with the relationship of the finite ego to the infinite matrix or source, if "relationship" be the right word.

Krishnamurti takes the physical existence of both observer and object for granted; or perhaps more accurately, he does not question their physical existence and refuses to be drawn into speculation on whether their ultimate nature is real or unreal. Since he is not concerned with erecting a new system of philosophy or in creating an all-embracing *Weltanschauung*, these questions are immaterial to him. What is more, dealing only with the immediate, practical aspects of living, Krishnamurti probably feels that to burden his teaching with various metaphysical issues would serve only to distract and confuse his listeners; and anyway that the clue to the problem of Being is divulged best through self-knowing, this rendering any intellectual discourse on such matters superfluous (in this connection, his attitude appears similar to that of Zen). In Maharshi's teaching, due to its different character, or rather its different approach, these considerations do not apply. This is because an examination of the nature of physical reality forms an integral and essential part of his teaching from its

71

very beginning and therefore does not act as a distracting or confusing element.

Thus, the apparent contradiction between the two teachings can be seen as due to a confusion of psychological and physical levels. To Krishnamurti, the ego is born from moment to moment with the state of inattention (duality), but it is possible—by being totally aware—not to nurture the desire-activated and desire-bound entity, which he calls the "observer." When thus the observer as a psychological entity has been transcended, there remains of course the observer as a physical entity; but this, falling outside the scope of his teaching, is not studied any deeper.

In Maharshi's teaching, the observer has extended duration for intermittent periods and has come into being through identification of consciousness with the body; once this consciousness sees itself as an "observer," it sees the world as objects having form and name. In Krishnamurti's teaching also, the primary nonpsychological component of the observer has been very clearly described as the formation of a "center of recognition" entailing the sequence perception, memory, and naming. Functioning as we do, and communicating, in relativity, this kind of observer has a necessary life of its own; but in the state of awareness it will not give rise to any psychological superstructure and thus not contribute to our bondage any longer. (The mountain is once again seen as a mountain, yet the quality of seeing has radically changed; at first when the mountain was perceived, it was simply "seeing"; then the action became "nonseeing"; and finally, it comprises both "seeing" and "nonseeing.")

Maharshi admonishes us to pursue constantly the inquiry "Who am I?" "To whom is this happening?" and so on, not because there is such a "Who," but because in the very search we shall discover its unreality—and this discovery puts an immediate end to the prevailing ego-sense. Since the observer as a psychological entity is nothing but a stream of thoughts, which is activated and maintained by desire, it can be readily seen that an examination of what is happening to that entity by pursuing the inquiry "Who am I?" must be essentially the same as the process of self-knowing in choiceless awareness. Both teachings have as common denominator the injunction: "Find out who is the observer, and everything will follow naturally from there."

Finally, regarding the "practicing" of awareness as a "spiritual exercise" at set times, we might ask, "Who is it that practices awareness?" If it is done through exertion of will, if I say to myself, "I am going to listen to what my mind tells me," then I have created the "listener," the observer, and therefore duality, which does not allow of choiceless awareness. True meditation does not tolerate any feedback. If you are conscious you are listening to music, then you are not all-listening. Similarly, if you are consciously engaged in being aware, you are *not* aware, you are in a state of duality.

It may now be clear that what constitutes one's practicing ground is the whole of everyday living, which includes the really testing situations, and not only when the mind is "under observation" and therefore at its best behavior. And why stay awake for only part of the day? Why let inattention create more problems than are necessary? If one sees the urgency of the matter, every moment counts; then one will naturally live every day as though it were one's last.

Sincerely,
R.P.

Postscript

After writing the above letter, the author would like to make some further observations which may serve to see Krishnamurti's and Ramana Maharshi's teachings in their proper perspectives. In this connection, he is particularly concerned with the issue that seems, as it were, the "un-common" denominator in both teachings: the relativity, or unreality, of all existence. This was obviously taken by Ramana Maharshi from the *Maya* doctrine of Hinduism and revitalized and elucidated by him in an extraordinary way. (This doctrine holds that the mind's sole capacity is "maya," which means "to measure," but that it is incapable of perceiving the real.) It must be pointed out, however, that this part of Maharshi's teaching, for which there is no place in Krishnamurti's teaching, is always in conjunction with, and inseparable from, the inquiry "Who am I?" In other words, it never became just a "doctrine." It is my view that any such realization of the relativity of the world, to have any value at all, must ever be part and parcel of self-knowing. Otherwise, it remains a mere intellectual truth, a piece of scientific information: it does not touch us in our core. In the following paragraphs I shall elaborate on this view by examining various implications of the issue.

To state that this world, with all its travail and sorrow, is not real, since it has merely relative existence, is all right so far as it goes. The statement is possibly justified, in having some significance, when made by those who have gone into the matter deeply and in the very making of it realize that their words have only relative meaning. For, one might equally well have stated that the world is neither real nor unreal: after all, what do we mean by "real"? Do we, as beings of relative existence and therefore illusory nature,

74

possess an absolute yardstick to characterize the "real" (and, consequently, the "unreal")? And does not in the very posing of that question lie at once the answer? In a sense, we might say there is no interval between the question and the answer as is normally the case when thought is groping for the solution to a problem. But here, the answer is not to be constructed from memory, from knowledge, by thought; a simple "yes" or "no" is not at all relevant, since we are not dealing with an "either/or" type of proposition. Hence, our remark about the world being neither real nor unreal. But, in the light of our further exploration, we may now add as equally valid the proposition that the world is both real and nonreal. All of which goes to show that, unlike in formal logic, a statement can be both true and false at the same time!

This kind of logical absurdity or paradox results only too frequently from an investigation into fundamental questions; here the laws of logic seem not only to be inoperative but irrelevant. It reminds one of how, when trying to solve a mathematical equation, any kind of absurd or meaningless answer may be obtained when dividing or multiplying by either Infinity or Zero. [Significantly, these are the parameters pointing to something fundamental in the physical world of space-time, for do they not stand for, respectively, the All ("existence") and Nothingness ("nonexistence") which, as we have already seen, are essentially identical? In fact, they are the only *absolute* mathematical entities one can think of; all others are quite obviously of a relative nature, since the very concept of "number" implies duality.]

The above discourse affords, to my mind, a glaring example—if any were still needed—of the impotence of speculative philosophy in embracing Reality. It also illustrates very well what happens when a true insight is verbalized—inevitably, this verbalization takes place with wholly inadequate tools—subsequently to be presented as "doctrine." In other words, the very process of verbalization has introduced a distorting, and therefore misleading, element. The doctrine is then advanced as a means to liberation. In the present case, we are told that the whole world is an illusion, a trick by the mind, like seeing a rope for a snake. One's sorrow, and so forth, does not really exist, so why worry?—the assumption here being that upon hearing this, we should be able to snap out of it at once (you know the old cliché about how the truth liberates). But, it seems to me, herein lies a fallacy. To the person who makes the statement it may be perfectly true: one has seen the relativity of all existence, including the nothingness and unreality of what one calls "self"; and this realization alone was sufficient to wipe out all self-pity and conflict. But to the individual who merely accepts such a statement as a valid concept, without having lived with the question and gone to the very end of it, it represents only so many words. Not having seen the unreality of self, to him the self is absolute, the world is absolute, and his sorrow is truly "his," and therefore not relative at all but deadly real. After all, until the snake is seen to be a rope, the snake is entirely real to the observer, engendering all the appropriate reactions of fear. (And we *must* have those reactions; they are natural, having survival value in cases where our observation *is* accurate and we are faced with real danger. The *Maya* doctrine is not going to change that and interfere with normal functioning on the nonpsychological level, unless it is to become a doctrine of *Nihilism*, which was by no means the intention of its founders.) Therefore, to tell someone who is

76

in mental agony that the world is unreal is meaningless. It is like telling a starving man that he does not need food, since neither the food nor his body are real. Whether the world is absolute or relative, there is still this world; and the fact remains that we have to deal with it, and with nothing else.

11

Questions
and
Answers

(This chapter is a record of certain questions and answers that came up during recent private discussion meetings held in New York and California. They are reproduced here in the belief that they may be of wider interest.)

Q *In one of your books you stated that Time equals Thought, equals Memory equals A property of the protoplast to retain physico-chemical changes in its substance. Could you elaborate on this, please?*

A It is really very simple: Without memory there could be no thought. Memory, recognition, is dependent upon the capacity of certain living tissues to "store" a stimulus. In this respect, the brain cells which are the physical counterpart of our faculty of memory are much like the tape recording without which the tape recorder is useless. The replay of this stimulus creates the concept of the past; the distance or space between imprinting and replay is "duration," time.

What is "recognition"? And how does one equate thought with time? I have an experience in the present, which I associate through memory with a past experience and I say: It is the same, similar, or different from that previous experience. These are the very elements of thought. Simultaneously with thought, desire is brought about. If the first experience was associated with pleasure, "recognition" renews my pleasure, but in a vague, secondhand sort of way; and I want more of the original experience, to regain my first taste of it.

Similarly with pain, but here I wish to escape, to forget; therefore, it can be seen that the mechanism of "forgetting" is not merely the opposite of "remembering"—it is part and parcel of it. It is remembering, but in a negative way. Perhaps we never really forget anything at all. But, because pleasure and pain are associated with every experience, remembering is never free from interference by the force of desire. It is therefore never a simple matter of "losing" some engram, but more like the tip of an iceberg that has moved out of sight, perhaps only temporarily.

Q   *Is it correct to say that Time can be divided into chronological time, biological time, and psychological time? And how do you see their interrelationship?*

A   Biological (or physiological) time is based on periodicity, on cyclic processes and events in living organisms, affording a measure of chronological time, just as

79

periodic events do in the world of physics and astronomy.

However, of relevance to the psyche is only what we have called elsewhere psychological time, the tension between what *is* and what *should be*. The effort by the psyche to bridge this gap is Time in the psychological sense.

One factor that all three forms of Time have in common is their dependency upon the existence of a highly evolved sensory-nervous system (which includes the brain), capable of receiving and processing information in digital form. This system must have the power to retain experience (Memory), and flowing from this, the capacity to conceive various abstract ideas (such as past, present, and future). In the ultimate, it is really this whole perceptive-evaluative apparatus, and its basically digital mode of operation, that creates Time; and absolutely speaking, all three categories of Time are illusory. But whereas both chronological and biological time are inherent to our essential physical and physiological state of being, psychological time is a superstructure created solely by the discursive intellect and is the cause of all bondage. That is why it is so very necessary to understand this question of Time.

Q   *What is the Way of Life, and how does one live from day to day?*

A   It is only us, unenlightened people, who are confused, have lost our way—who demand a plan to guide us through life. Where there is enlightenment there is Love, and to have this Love is to be eternally in the light, so that there is never any darkness, any obscurity, on our path, and therefore no need for guidance.

When we are confused, we are easily tempted to look up to the man who has a blueprint, a prescription, for the happy life; and there will be thousands of these persons who are only too keen to sell it to us— the philosophers, psychologists, religionists, and frauds— but if we accept any of their crutches, we shall be worse off and even more confused.

It seems to me that our problem is not that of guidance at all, but rather that of "choice." Only when we must choose, do we look toward guidance—either from the experience of others, our own; or from God. And for a mind that is totally uncommitted, a mind that is truly empty of thought, is there choice? Not having any psychological problems and therefore never faced with choice, it is ever capable of an immediate action which springs from the observation of what *is*.

On the other hand, the mind that is burdened with a problem is an inefficient mind; all its energies go into decision making, and it has none left for clear perception. Living in contradiction, there is ever a gap between thought and action; and that action is always tainted with frustration. Whereas the empty mind acts, the burdened mind merely reacts from its frustration.

Freedom is incompatible with Choice; and for a conditioned entity there is always a choice to be made. To that entity, it is an apparent instance of exercising its Free Will (a flagrant misnomer), but in actual fact it is a wholly determined action. Therefore, in order to live from day to day, the mind must rediscover its Freedom afresh each day.

Q *Why is there no fundamental change in the world?*
A As he has created God, so Man has created the world

81

in his own image. That world is the product of his fears, illusions, hopes, conflicts, and so on. Where we see wars, cruelty, exploitation of every kind going on in the world, these are but the projections of what is within the mind of man. Hence, the real crisis lies not in the World, but in Consciousness. Only after a complete change of heart in the individual can there be a different world.

But one of the greatest hindrances to such a fundamental change is that we are noncognizant of the above-stated fact. Man takes the World very much for real—he has not the capacity to discriminate between the Real and the Illusory. Hence, he sits back and expects the World to change—not himself; all this is part of man's psychological inertia.

As long as man pursues the same goals he has been pursuing for thousands of years—essentially based on self-aggrandizement, forming the animalistic part of his being—there can obviously be no change. Change can only come with the essential perception of the emptiness of "things," and the realization that we are the makers of duality.

Q *In your book* Crisis in Consciousness (*page 121*) *you state that all things are of Thought; and that there is no Matter as opposed to Thought. Would you please clarify this further?*

A We only comprehend through comparison, correlation, of concepts, symbols, and so forth. This is the manner of thought, and any conception of ultimate Reality which we can have is through Thought. But that conception of Reality must necessarily be contaminated by the limitation of thought. It is like looking at the World through colored spectacles: the picture will always bear testimony to the presence of the glasses. And if we are not conscious of wearing spectacles, then that picture of the world will to us be real.

Similarly, our conception of Reality will always be circumscribed by duality, thought, thus leading to a mere abstraction; and if we have not probed the whole mechanism of thinking in great depth, then that abstraction will seem to us to be the Real.

To go further than this in our search—that is, not to be held by the intellectual conceptions and abstractions —is possible, but for that we must first fully understand how duality operates, how we conceptualize. This is not mysticism, but forms part of the process of self-knowing, which holds the clue to any form of knowing, because in it one discovers that the self is not different from the not-self.

In the passage in the book I tried to indicate that all concepts, entities, "things," result from experiencing in space-time, which is essentially the particular mode of our thinking. None of these things is therefore ultimately real, but all belong to thought. You may add them, subtract them, manipulate them in whatever way you like, but all that will never bring forth Reality. Even their interrelatedness is what Thought itself has imposed on them; it is coincident with the very naming, defining, of the entities.

Take for instance "matter"; this has value only as an empirical concept, but on a fundamental basis such conceptualization becomes a waste of time. In the very naming, thought has created matter; therefore, it is neither wholly true to say that it is identical nor that it is nonidentical with thought.

The ultimate Reality, although not cognizable by or

within thought, has been named, variously, as Non-duality, the One, and so forth. In certain Oriental writings it has been designated as Mind (Note the capital M). This has nothing to do, and must not be confused with, the mind of man as creator of duality. In one way, one may consider it an ill-chosen name because of its potential for confusion. On the other hand, one feels, it may have been chosen—at least, in part—to counteract the school of philosophy, particularly prevalent in the West, which views the ultimate Reality as Matter, and the mind as being secondary, accidental, and irrelevant to the existence of the material world.

Q *What is the relationship, if any, between the socially accepted "morality" and the Morality which is not man-made?*

A At present, morality is based entirely on thought, ideation, precept. Since, as we have already seen, thought is the product of a particular culture, together with various other conditioning factors, morality is ever a thing of space and time; it has nothing absolute about it. And being merely a system of ethics, a set of rules as to how to play the social game, the word "morality" is really a misnomer.

   Morality is devised by a particular society to maintain itself as it is. In this connection, the most active part in upholding morality is played by those elements in that society who hold most power and who have therefore most to lose in any upheaval of values. This means that such morality is ever tainted by hypocrisy: the rules of conduct are laid down primarily for "others" and not for oneself. Is it not a fact that morality is always used as a weapon by the more conservative forces within society, as a counterforce to "change"?

Freedom, paradoxically, brings its own discipline and its own Morality, but these are not "imposed." They are not yet another set of rules, the result of ideation, but are inherent in that Freedom. And as such they bear no relationship whatever to the values of Society.

Q *At some time you have stated or implied that the psychological structure of Society is based not on sanity but insanity. What would you say is the worst feature of such insanity?*

A The worst sign of insanity is perhaps that Society flies in the face of Death. Why? Because its worship of success, fame, and private property is in direct contradiction to the recognition of our real nature, which may perhaps be represented by the triad Nothingness/Transiency/Vulnerability. The religious Establishment talks glibly about "eternal values," but in this connection "eternity" stands for "permanency"; and that is why Society enjoins us to go in for the accumulation of every kind of goods—material, intellectual, and even what it calls "spiritual." To one, however, who has perceived the Emptiness of self (and of nonself), such values are all worldly, or unreal, and therefore "unspiritual."

So, based on this monumental delusion, man devotes his life to the acquisition of those things which have no value, and in doing so he is always in battle with his fellow beings. For make no mistake about it, such a Society can only be ruthlessly competitive on all levels; it nurtures the attitude of "every man for himself,"

85

which is euphemistically called "private enterprise."

It is suggested that no good can ever come from a Society that refuses to face Reality; it is like building a house on shifting sands. There is just no possibility of reconciling a way of life essentially based on violence, conflict, with the need and potential of human beings to flower in goodness: where competition and ambition prevail, there can be no peace and cooperation among men. We may occasionally find instances of cooperation among people at war under the threat of a common enemy, but never cooperation *and* peace at the same time.

The question whether Society is incapable of recognizing Reality, or whether it merely runs away from it after glimpsing some of its unpalatable truths, is a valid one but of secondary importance, since the end result is the same. If the latter be the case, Society may well harden in its attitude of clinging to false values as being a giant escape reaction from what is Real. After all, Society reflects, and acts for, the Ego—and the ego and Reality cannot possibly coexist.

Q   *In* Crisis in Consciousness (*page 130*) *you mention the birth of "thingness" as being the origination of Duality. My question now is: How does the mind create "thingness"?*

A   Maya (to measure) stands for Illusion, and Man is the measure of all things. A fly, for example, sees an entirely different world and a bat perceives a sound "picture" of its surroundings; there is more than beauty alone in the eye and mind of the beholder.

So, the world which Man perceives is as much the

result of his own psycho-physiological make-up, as that of the world's self-nature (if there be any). As we have shown elsewhere,* the "thing in itself" does not really exist; it is ever in relationship to an observer, and it is the latter that endows the observed with reality as a "thing" or entity.

After all, to create "thingness" is to measure, to limit; it is to erect some "thing" in a space-time frame of reference. This is what the "eye-brain" system is ever engaged in doing, converting digital nerve impulses into three-dimensional entities. With the images, come thought, desire, and so forth. Therefore, space-time, or "thingness," is not separate from the mind. It is part and parcel of our thought, but we suffer from the illusion that space-time is something external to the mind. (See also Chapter 22, page 178, of the afore-mentioned book.)

Coincident with becoming aware of duality (that is, the self and the not-self, and subsequently, the myriads of "entities" of the outside world), this fact finds expression in the process of "naming." Language at once confirms and perpetuates duality, our particular mode of consciousness.

Q *You've stated somewhere, and I have heard it said elsewhere, that although body and mind appear different, in reality they are one. Can you show me why they are basically identical?*

A It would be just as difficult for me to prove their identity as it would be for you to demonstrate that their apparent differences are real; but in certain areas of

* (*Crisis in Consciousness,* page 108.)

interest it is more important to see something for oneself than to be persuaded of it by others.

Orthodox science still generally considers mind and matter, and therefore also mind and body, as belonging to entirely different realms, and most of us have been brought up to accept this, or we do not question it. However, as is almost universally the case, things are not what they appear to be. For, what is the real nature of mind, and the real nature of matter? We can perhaps typify mind by reciting some of its characteristics, and we may do the same for matter—but do we know what they *are*? We may say, for example, that matter consists of such and such particles, which in turn are composed of other smaller particles, and so on; but all these are explanations in terms of the known, and we have still not answered the question what matter is, what mind is (or anything else).

Our conclusion then must be that, since we do not know what either mind or matter is, we are not entitled to denote the separation implied in the words— and words *always* cut up reality—as the "final word" in the matter.Words simply beg the question because they reflect—and this is how they have come into being —appearances. On a certain level, this is only too obvious; for example, we all know that steam and ice are both composed of water, however different their appearances. But the problem goes much deeper. Therefore, to find out anything original, we have to break out of this vicious circle and penetrate beyond the verbal level.

So far, our discussion has been entirely negative, almost agnostic. However, it seems to me that some simple facts of experience may indicate where the truth lies. First, I would like to pose the following question: If body and mind do indeed belong to entirely different spheres, would it be possible for them to be in constant, close interaction? In fact, would it be possible for them to interact even to the slightest extent? Now the truth of the matter is that in a normal healthy individual there appear to exist the fullest possible cooperation and almost complete interaction between body and mind. Every moment of conscious activity testifies to this: for example, the mere thought—my mental decision—to stretch out my legs produces (or, better, is accompanied by) a stretching-out movement of the legs—a little miracle which is normally taken for granted, despite the prevalent outlook upon thought power as being utterly intangible, almost ethereal, and therefore far removed from something as grossly material as muscle power. Physiologists have found that even on a less conscious level, such as in dreaming or daydreaming, the mere thought of a bodily action has its counterpart in a corresponding muscle twitching, however minute. Also, by this same mysterious thought power, chemicals and other changes are brought about: I only have to think of some appetizing food for the mouth to secrete saliva. Think also of the close interaction between mental life and hormonal activity. Many other miracles of such remote-controlled operations could be mentioned here, some of which we have simply accepted and others we make a great deal of fuss over, saying: "Mind over matter!" Maybe, however, the true miracle is "Mind *with* matter!"

Now, it would be possible at this stage to oversimplify

the issue and say: Every thought is accompanied by electrical changes in the brain cells, and it is these electrical phenomena that are ultimately responsible for triggering off muscular contractions. Because if you did, you would again be begging the question. Movements of electricity are material phenomena, and the question therefore remains: How do these electrical changes come into being through no apparent physical cause?

At this stage of my inquiry I feel obliged to posit: Either matter is not quite what I imagined it to be, or thought is not quite what I imagined it to be—or both propositions must hold true.

Now either body and mind belong to different orders of reality and then could have no points of contact, and therefore any interaction would be an impossibility; or they are not inherently different at all, in which case there may be certain meeting points between them making interaction possible.

Let me use some analogies to elucidate the situation. For a force to be effective in moving an object upon which it is acting, there must be some point of attack or "fulcrum"; from this requirement it follows that it is only "like" that can effectively act upon "like." For example, light can interact with light, sound with sound, but light waves and sound waves do not interact. Propulsion of a sailing boat is made possible by the fact that its sails "catch" the wind and utilize the latter's kinetic energy, but these same sails are unable to utilize the energy of a so-called "magnetic storm" (which, incidentally, is not a storm at all but comprises intense magnetic fields, associated with high sunspot activity).

The fact, therefore, that body and mind interact so

closely affords me a strong indication that they are not really different on a deeper, not-visible level. And if they are not different, then *inherently* they must be identical, like two sides of a coin. Once we can accept this for fact, it will throw a new light on many phenomena, such as psychosomatic disease and pain. Henceforth we shall be able to view a human being as a psychosomatic unity rather than a dual entity possessed of a body and a mind.

There are also other, less reasoned approaches toward seeing this truth—and in a total manner. For example, we can penetrate the appearance of *all* duality, which is our *Maya*, by carefully going into the phenomenon of perception, beginning with the nature of the "percipient."

Q *In trying to be "choicelessly aware," I find it very difficult to withhold judgment. I believe this to be a major difficulty for most people in the West who are doing this practice of observation, so conditioned and brainwashed as they have been since childhood with the Judeo-Christian ethic.*

A In the West people are conditioned by one thing, in the East by another, but the particular content of their conditioning has no relevance to the issue. The fact is that we are no longer human beings, but conditioned entities whose actions have become psychological reflexes, and therefore, highly mechanical. And all conditioning, of whatever nature, prevents the seeing of things as they are.

Now, sir, first of all, may I ask you why you want to be aware? Do you wish to be aware because in doing

91

so you hope to achieve something? Or do you wish to be aware because you clearly see the urgent necessity for it? Is awareness something about which you've heard but which is really no part of your ordinary experience, or is it part and parcel of being alive?

At present most of our activities are the results of external pressures, or of the prospect of some reward—in other words, the whip and the carrot. There are relatively few things one does without motivation; a labor of love has become an extremely rare thing these days. Choiceless awareness must be such a thing, done out of love; otherwise it is senseless. It is not a mechanical activity, not a discipline imposed on you, not yet one more struggle that has an end in view, a reward; but if you make it into that, and it then becomes another routine practice—because you have a motive to achieve some goal—it will no longer be "choiceless awareness" but a process of resistance and a waste of energy. I happen to know a lady who "practices awareness," but only when unpleasant things are closing in on her; she finds it a perfect escape mechanism, but she does not realize the lopsided nature of her activity, namely, the attempt to do away with pain, while retaining all pleasure. In other words, she is trying to have her spiritual cake and eat it. Although she herself talks theoretically a great deal about "transcending opposites," and ought therefore to know better, in reality her "spiritual exercise" is only another form of conditioned reflex.

Other people I know like to squash their conditioning by making a frontal attack on it; but this is the way of violence and can therefore result only in more struggle.

Because every action breeds its own reaction, such people will only succeed in swapping one form of conditioning for another, like the Roman Catholic who becomes a militant atheist, or vice versa. Our conditioning, being the very nature of our brain cells, cannot be destroyed or neutralized by any action; it can only be bypassed. Once you bypass it, as in choiceless awareness, you no longer give strength to that conditioning, and it can then wither away naturally. How does one bypass one's conditioning? By exposing it to oneself. In such exposure, is there then still an *entity* that is conditioned? The entity exists only so long as you are being activated, manipulated, by your particular background. So, to bypass one's conditioning is rather like overcoming an adversary by nonfighting—a kind of mental Judo.

In sum, choiceless awareness has to come into being without any pressure by the mind, spontaneously; otherwise, it is not "choiceless." Therefore, first go into the question of motivation, and find out whether your choiceless awareness is a means to an end, or whether it is an end in itself to you. If the latter be the case, the right foundation will be present. Then, do not try to "withhold judgment," for such a thing is not really possible; if you tried it you would only repress thought and strengthen the subconscious mind. Do not even *try* to be aware—just *be* it. Experiment with it, play with it, and see what happens; nobody can tell you, and if anyone did it would be of little value to you. But, above all, do not make a problem of it; we have already enough problems as it is.

Be passively aware of all that passes in front of the mind's eye, and when an object arouses "judgment," let

93

it be—just be aware of *that*. Please see that all acts of mentation are equally important or unimportant, whether it be the first mental observation or a subsequent one, a "second thought"; in other words, in awareness there is no discrimination of any kind and thus no need to single out, to repress or to exalt a thought, however "noble" or "vile" it might be labeled by judgment; and each thought is observed separately at any particular time, because there is no retention of mentation by means of memory.

When thus aware of every observation and its possible reactions, associations, and so on, from moment to moment without memorizing, and therefore without giving further impetus to thought, without creating any resistance between the seer and the seen, is there then any longer a censor at work who is judging according to the Judeo-Christian ethic, or whatever it may be? And without censor, is there still a center of conditioning? Then what happens? Without any conscious action on the part of the observer, the train of mental reflections and images has slowed down noticeably; at the same time the seeing has become most direct, most vivid, because it is no longer distorted by any form of conditioning. Such seeing leaves not even a trace in memory; it does not sow a seed of fresh conditioning.

Q *You and other writers talk about Truth—THE Truth—as though it were something unique and absolute. But am I not right in thinking that there is really no such thing as objective truth, that truth will always contain an element of subjectivity and therefore be dependent upon one's point of view?*

A In one way you are right, but in another way you are wrong. As long as we regard truth as knowledge or information, your assumption is correct. (Even scientific truth concerns only relativities and is therefore neither unique nor absolute.) But those of us who speak of THE Truth— and here at least I am speaking for myself—do not consider that it is possible to express this Truth in a religious doctrinal formula, such as "Thou art That," in a scientific formula (like $E = mc^2$) or in any philosophy of Man and the Universe, however comprehensive. And, come to think of it—or rather, not-think of it—I am not even sure whether there *is* a "Universe." (We are generally not aware what important silent assumptions are made when using this term.) I really do not know anything about such matters, and so shy away from those philosophies that attempt to discover, through exploration of astronomy (and astrology?), Truth as being some relationship between Man and the physical universe. And I feel similarly about attempts to learn the meaning of existence by relating Man to Time, that is, to some hypothesized evolutionary process. Generally, I prefer to stay closer to home and study the things pertaining to Man and with which I am therefore intimately involved; for example, the immediate facts of my experience like pain, pleasure, desire, attachment, and fear. Also I like to reflect on the little inferential knowledge that I possess of the brain, especially on its function as a complex computer which processes digital data in the form of nervous impulses. As long as I do not know my self and am learning about it, I feel not too concerned about the ultimate nature of cosmic realities.

Naturally, I am not saying that there is no place for such studies as astronomy and cosmology, but not as a means of finding the key to Reality; this key still lies within oneself and not out there.*

To me, all attempts to express the Truth are like trying to contain the waters of the ocean within a bucket. Such renditions of (the) truth as have been made are at best exercises in symbology—and let us remember that all symbols are ultimately the brain's own creations—and at worst verbalized analogies of fragmentary verities. But if you mean by Truth an insight, an understanding, an experience not yet verbalized and thereby translated into something else, then I think you are wrong. The trouble is that to us language has become so terribly important—and undeniably, it *is* important on a certain level, as a specific function of communication—that sometimes we forget that our world of living and experiencing is inherently nonverbal and nonsymbolic. That is, we tend to forget—if we have ever realized it—that the word is not the thing, and more importantly, that the word always stands in the way of total understanding. When we "understand" a sequence of words or symbols, there is understanding of some sort, but it is and always remains a partial understanding; and this fragmentary understanding may block the total comprehension which comes with the direct, nonverbal, and nonsymbolic vision.

As happens so frequently when we do not see eye to

---

* Alan Bean, after returning from his successful moon voyage, said the one great disappointment of his experience was that it had given him no revelation regarding the problem of Man in the Universe and his relationship to God.

eye in a discussion, more often than not any differences are basically caused by semantic ambiguities or obscurities; so also it is in this case, for what exactly do we mean by "truth"? Do we mean truth as knowledge or truth as understanding? The confusion is further compounded for some of us by the fact that in certain Oriental writings (for example, Buddhist) the term "right knowledge" is often used in a specific sense. It does not signify simply "correct data" or "useful information," but is really *a way of seeing*, an essential insight into a situation—especially one that concerns oneself in relationship at any particular moment. "Right knowledge" is more accurately a way of living, of understanding, in which at each moment one observes the world with an innocent eye. And paradoxically, it is found that in such perception, in which the observer has emptied himself of all knowledge and experience, one can see something as true or false, unfailingly—and in an instant. "Right knowledge" is therefore really "no-knowledge," and I feel that the effort religious writers sometimes make to differentiate "innocence" from "ignorance" is largely unnecessary and is probably due to the unfavorable associations of the term "ignorance" in a Society that sets a high premium on "knowledge." (The philosophy of "knowledge is power" seems the very antipode of the wisdom of the Zen Idiot!) For when I wish to learn about anything, should I not be totally free from preconceived ideas that might interfere with my observation, and also, because the little I know may be completely incorrect or irrelevant? Therefore, must I not first say, "I do not know," so that I may be in a state of maximum receptivity? Even in the spiritual sphere, or especially there, it seems that "A little learning is a dangerous thing!"

Again, the situation is further confounded by the fact that in the East the term "Avidya" or Ignorance means not so much "want of knowledge" (which is the definition of "ignorance" given by the *Oxford English Dictionary*) as "want of understanding."

So, Truth and knowledge belong to different dimensions. I do not know if you have ever thought about it, but the self, with its immediate experience, is really all that exists. Is not everything else, the whole world, contained in that? In saying this, I may sound like a case of megalomania to you, but don't reject it offhand; go into it very carefully and you will see it for yourself. In a very deep sense we must affirm, then, that "Man is the measure of all things." Therefore, we must understand man, the only yardstick, which means that to us the measure and the measured, the observer and the observed, the thinker and the thought are one. What we are saying is not something mystical or supernatural, but it signifies that at any instant there can be a completeness in a simple vision of the self in relationship: it is our only reality.

Truth can only be hinted at, pointed to, but never conveyed. To ask "What is Truth?" is not a legitimate question and has no meaning whatsoever if you expect to be told. It is only legitimate when you put the question to yourself. Any verbalization or pictorialization of Truth has relevance and validity only in a negative sense: "Not this, not this . . ." That is why it is so silly to argue about the Truth as one can over truth in the more limited sense of the word. Truth is a private experience, yet the perception is neither subjective nor objective, neither individual nor universal in its validity. The moment of truth is a moment of liberation, in which there is neither the self nor the nonself; it is the end of all categorizing and therefore the beginning of Silence.

Q *Some years ago, as part of an effort to explore the unknown and to understand myself better, I went to Mexico to participate in several "mushroom agape" rites (that is, consuming mushrooms containing the psychedelic chemical psilocybin). On those occasions I saw very forcefully the phony or negative side of my nature. However, even this very forceful "seeing" did not purge me at once of ambition and greed. I do not think, therefore, that awareness frees one from these states immediately, as Krishnamurti appears to indicate. I rather feel that it is possible only to diminish their hold over us by persistently carrying out these "here-and-now" exercises in self-observation over a considerable period of time.*

A I wonder why we go to such extraordinary lengths in order to see the petty nature of the ego and its overall activities! And why is simply being aware such a problem for many of us? As to gradualism as a way to liberation, we have discussed this topic so many times, that we will not go into it again at this moment.

I think that implicit in your statement is a very important question, namely, whether or not there can be a fundamental change in the quality of one's life, and if so how to set about bringing it about. And by "fundamental change" is not meant a mere modification or embellishment of the personality, but a complete breaking up of the old personality which reflects itself in the making of a clean break with one's past. Thus it constitutes a real turning point in one's life course, and the term "rebirth" may not be inappropriate in this connection.

It seems to me that if we are in fact undergoing such a rebirth as the result of a complete clarification of mind, then the question as to whether or not it will be a lasting change has no meaning at all. This question arises only so long as self-observation has been partial, fragmentary, and consequently of fuzzy clarity, although to the observer it may well appear as a revelation of dazzling brilliance. The difficulty, for most of us, lies in seeing anything totally—the very key to "awareness." You know, occasionally all of us do see in total fashion, with full clarity; for example, when threatened with great danger in a crisis. When I have only a split second to act, and therefore absolutely no time to think it over, the mind suddenly falls silent and at the same time all the senses are in a state of heightened sensitivity. It may be that I am walking and suddenly realize that I am heading straight for a steep precipice. Do I not halt immediately? Do I have to look repeatedly to convince myself of the necessity to turn away from my dangerous course? Of course not. Now all this can be true no less in other, noncrisis situations if we know the art of being aware. Strictly speaking, awareness cannot be learned, but it becomes a possibility when we understand what takes place when we are *not* aware.

To be aware means to see something totally, so that

there can be an immediate action without equivocation. And to perceive totally is a seeing without the observer, with all his ideation, interfering with the vision. Such seeing, being an impersonal process, does not entail the emotions (which are part of the observer) and thus cannot be measured in intensity as "very forceful" or otherwise. Nor is it fragmentary, as when you differentiate between the "positive" and the "negative" side of your self. Who, anyway, decides what is "positive" or "negative," "good" or "bad," etc., if not the observer decreeing this from his background? As I have stated before, "choiceless awareness" is to observe out of silence, that is, without judgment, without emotion, and without categorizing; this leaves absolutely no place for the observer (who is the eternal censor). Rather than a "learning," awareness entails an "unlearning," namely, an unlearning of the conditioned reflexes of the observer. Unlike most "learning"/"unlearning" processes, however, this particular "unlearning" does not entail discipline or repression.

Now supposing, being aware in this sense, I have seen deeply into my identity, and know therefore what I am—or rather, what I am *not*—do I then carry on as though nothing has happened? Does my conduct remain as though I still believe (and therefore live) in my previous, mistaken identity? Or is there an immediate cessation of all searching, and of all efforts to achieve something as a means of personal fulfillment?

I know I may have raised more questions than I have answered, but let each of us experiment with "awareness"; you won't know the answers until you have actually done it.

Q *On page 30 of* "Crisis in Consciousness" *you state:* ". . . *having seen myself as I really am, is there not a purgation all at once?*" *I wonder if Krishnamurti does not appear to contradict this (*Madras Talks, 1953, *page 59):* "*Reality comes into being after a great deal of meditation—the meditation being the thinking out, watching, observing, not letting the mind to play tricks upon it. . . .*"

A It is always dangerous to lift a sentence or paragraph from a book or a talk and thus divorce it from its general context, especially when dealing with extremely subtle matters such as these. For one thing, it is usually possible to come up with a counterquotation that appears to prove the very opposite.* Whatever you may like to read into the above-quoted words by Krishnamurti, he hardly ever misses the opportunity to point out that gradualism is *not* the way to Reality, that time only breeds disorder and that when we depend on time to find the timeless we get hopelessly lost. He does so because he is well acquainted with our hang-ups, one of which is our dependence upon time!

Incidentally, all this illustrates so well the trouble one incurs with quotations, not so much in the field of science, technology, and the like, but while inquiring on a fundamental level into psychological questions. I am not against quotations, for on occasions I use

* E.g.: *First and Last Freedom* (p. 269): "To perceive truth needs no preparation; preparation implies time and time is not the means of understanding truth ... Understanding is non-continuous, it is from moment to moment, unresidual"; and from the Paris Talks, 1966 (p. 71): "It is only when time ends that creation takes place, and a mind that depends on yesterday, today and tomorrow as a means of achieving something lives in utter, hopeless despair."

102

them myself, but am concerned with the manner of their use. When we use quotations as our points of departure, their sources become our very authorities; and when we depend on authorities there is no longer any true inquiry—least of all self-inquiry. On the other hand, where there is no dependence on a quotation, but one simply adduces it to highlight an insight independently acquired, or to represent it verbally in a more apt way than one is capable of oneself, I cannot see that such quotation constitutes a hindrance to learning.

Again, coming back to your quotation from page 30 of my book, in comparing this with the text on page 90, you might detect a similar, apparent contradiction. If you would reread what was said on page 30, you will find that I was attempting to indicate the futility of any process to "train" the mind with a view toward its eventual transformation. Training implies a gradual improvement, or molding, based upon the following two factors: discipline and the mere passage of time. It is a possibility only if that which is to be improved has an essential continuity in time. Thus it is possible to train one's body and to train one's memory, the latter representing the part of the psyche that has continuity.

Self-discovery, on the other hand, is not a process of storing up information about oneself. It does not build upon the past, thus creating continuity, but it is the way of immediate understanding: the seeing of what one is, and of what *is*, at any particular moment. The flash of insight affords a completeness of vision, because it is no longer from a limited point of view, which has come about as the result of certain identifications. Such a vision is therefore free from resistance and does not lead to an interference with, as a reaction to, what is being perceived. Therefore, in the absence of the narrow viewpoint, which is the "I" and is responsible for such states as "ambition" and "greed," there is a momentary transformation. What else, then, could it be but a kind of "purgation all at once"?

On page 90 of the same book I was discussing the overall situation of someone who is aware for at least part of his waking life, in relation to the concept of "satori" as promulgated by Zen Buddhism. Generally, I am extremely reluctant to engage in deliberations on the nature of "satori"—whether there is "little satori" or "great satori," whether satori is reversible or irreversible, or even whether there is such a thing as "satori" at all. In the nature of things, I feel that such deliberations can only be speculations which, more often than not, are given in by a mistaken notion of continuity—by the idea that we have a definite, lasting identity—and by our hankering after permanency. I don't know whether you have ever thought it out completely, but it seems to me that if man is not a permanent psychological entity but the momentary manifestation of a thought process, then the very idea of an "enlightened being" becomes rather doubtful, if not altogether meaningless. "Enlightenment," yes, but an "enlightened person"? The latter would imply "having finally arrived," an irreversible achievement, a state of permanency; and how could this be when we know full well that there is nothing permanent in this world? Please don't misunderstand me; I am just investigating, not maintaining categorically that there is not or that there is the possibility of a so-called Enlightened One (or more, if you like). For must we not be constantly on our guard not to take anything for granted, so that from our own scrutiny we may discover whether a particular thesis becomes an actuality or remains a mere concept?

Personally, I feel and have stated elsewhere that a moment of clarity in awareness is not the final condition; it is really only the beginning of our learning process. For within and through these timeless moments of immediate perception there takes place a further movement; unlike the movements within limited consciousness, that is, within time, this movement does not appear to have a purpose or an end in view. This movement of deepening self-exploration is one in which Reality increasingly reveals itself, in which we seem to become increasingly part of this Reality; yet all this is a process in which time, and therefore thought, plays not the smallest part. But as soon as we start talking about these things, we are liable to become confused, because to us a word has certain definite associations; and when we speak of such a "movement" or "a great deal of meditation," the mind immediately seizes upon this terminology to quantify it, translating the expression as something that involves a greater or lesser amount of time. Also, if such a movement of meditation represents an endless journey, having, as Krishnamurti once said, a beginning but no end, can there be "satori"? And if all this is mistaken and the journey *has* an end after all, how is one ever to know? This is not something that can be worked out logically, or even guessed at. If it is not a personal certainty from direct experience, one could only have this knowledge secondhand, and then again it would imply the acceptance of authority with all its pitfalls.

Q *My problem is that I do not know whether, as Krishnamurti suggests, I should be totally involved with everything that goes on around me, or whether I should stay aloof from all that, and let the world take care of itself, as was admonished by the late Ramana Maharshi.*

A No, madam, that is an interpretation of fragments of these teachings that you are giving, and *any* interpretation—whether it's yours or mine—is wide of the mark and renders a disservice to the cause of truth. Why do we follow teachings? We do so because we want guidance, and these teachings appear to offer us just that—some tangible information which we only have to recognize, understand, and live by in order to reach our goal. However, the unfortunate truth is that as long as we cannot go beyond a verbal understanding of what, to us, seem like "ready-made conclusions," we shall always miss the real point of the teachings. On the other hand, if we are capable of penetrating more deeply and are no longer captivated by words and concepts, do we then still need any teachings? Teachings are words, formulae, and the moment I am beyond the verbal level—which really means beyond "duality"—I am in immediate contact with the world and actively learning about myself, not through a screen of words and ideas but directly; therefore I am already beyond all teachings.

Then, one might ask: What are teachings for? Any spiritual teacher worth his salt has only one aim, one mission: to make men doubt their present certainties, to cleanse them of any bourgeois mentality (the word "bourgeois" here being used in its nonpolitical meaning) and to awaken in them a true spirit of inquiry. In this inquiry, which is its own, tremendous discipline, nothing is taken for granted and no facts are interpreted or judged according to one's preconceived ideas, likes, or dislikes. Thus the "teaching" itself has no immediate utility in the matter of our deliverance. But if it comes from a truly enlightened source, it may hit us in our weak spots; acting like a catalyst, it may then trigger off a process of learning which enables us to stand on our own feet for the first time in our lives and do without teacher altogether. Perhaps what I have tried to convey here illuminates in some way Ramana Maharshi's dictum: "The real *guru* is within." He is within everyone of us, and to discover this truth is really what meditation is all about. And by that much-abused term I do not mean the phony kind of meditation that aims at cultivating a certain mystical state of mind—a kind of self-hypnosis—or meditation as "concentration," which consists in the discipline of pinpoint focusing the attention on some trivial item. This is not the place to go into the subject in depth, but meditation is perhaps best hinted at by stating that it is a process of "preverbal inquiry" which, as common sense dictates, should begin with an examination of the inquirer himself. And because the inquiry is prior to verbalization, one sees in silence what *is*, without the noise distraction of what *should be*.

After this digression, let us take a fresh look at the

107

question of involvement, this time without accepting guidance from any source. When we say "We must get involved," what does it really mean? It implies, does it not, that at present we are in a condition which is the very opposite and might be described more or less adequately as one of "isolation" or "separation."

Now it seems to me that, whether we do anything about it or not, and whether we like it or not, we are already totally involved in many essential ways, perhaps without realizing it. First, is it not a fact that on the vegetative level of our existence we function not at all as isolated entities but as beings totally integrated with our physical environment and without necessitating any conscious effort? Everything there happens as though we are part of something much greater, and without direction by some supervising entity which we call the "self." In fact, the very opposite appears to be true: as soon as the brain tries to interfere with the autonomic processes of the body we are asking for trouble. Quite obviously these processes are perfectly capable of looking after themselves: the body seems to possess a wisdom all its own. On other occasions I have tried to indicate that as a physical and physiological entity, man's separateness is merely empirical—that fundamentally it is an illusion, notwithstanding the apparent boundary of the skin.

Then what about man as a psychological organism? Here again, it seems to me that the real situation is very different from the apparent picture with which we are so familiar. As psychological and social beings, whether we like it or not, are we not already totally dependent upon, and therefore involved with, Society and the world in which we live? Is not the entire Universe interrelated and are we not constantly relating to, and interacting with, our environment? And also, have we not observed that what matters most in Nature is the maintenance of this interrelatedness, the balance of Life, of which the survival of the species is an important part; and that what we call the "individual" (that is, the "separate" entity) has relatively minor importance?

How then has the idea arisen that we must become involved? The idea, obviously, has arisen because we hold on to the *concept* of our being separate entities and live according to that concept; the opposite, to be non-separate, which is to be no-thing, seems like the ultimate death. In other words, although inherently totally submerged in Life, in Consciousness, and therefore "involved," psychologically we create our own (artificial) separateness and struggle to maintain it. That is, based on an idea of separateness, of being non-involved, we create images of ourselves and of others; and as we have seen on previous occasions, as long as there is the interplay of these images we do not truly relate to each other. Then, dimly sensing our artificial state of isolation, expressing itself as a deep feeling of loneliness, futility (which is really our frustration in seeing no meaning, no purpose, in living) and despair, we ask: Must I not get "involved"? And underlying the question one hears the agonized cry of a human being seeking fulfillment, by whatever means.

The problem, therefore, seems to me not how to get involved, but rather how to reverse the process of isolation in which we constantly escape from facing up

109

to life; how to stop erecting barriers of self-enclosing memories that emphasize our illusion of separateness. In this connection, is it not ironical that, excluded as we are from the main stream of Consciousness, we ever strive to become even more "exclusive"? To be "ordinary," that is, nondifferentiated, appears to us an unmitigated horror and misfortune.

The truth must eventually dawn upon us that there is neither the individual as against Society, nor Society as against the individual, but that these are merely like the two sides of the same coin. And therefore, when one does not cultivate one's own backyard and really lives without self-defensiveness—which means that one is completely vulnerable and never runs away from anything—in that state of let-go one *is* involved simply by being what is one's true nature; and the question of *becoming* involved therefore never arises.

Let me restate the problem somewhat. Most of us are engaged in fostering our separateness, by various forms of escape and self-nourishing activities; and when some pressure is put upon us (that is, when our autonomy, which is our separateness, our self-interest, is threatened), we take the line of least resistance—we conform, we become "yes-men." When we see evil being committed in the name of God, the nation, humanity, justice, or whatever it may be, it is much easier and "safer" to say "yes" or to keep quiet (which is only another form of "yes-saying"). But when we cease to function within the limitations of our self-concern, we shall find that we have become "no-men" spontaneously and without fear. Then we shall be "turned-on" in the most fundamental sense of the word, that is, tuned in to Life, the whole of it and not just that part which gives us a little pleasure or provides us some security. Even the very idea of being "no-men," of going against the prevailing trend, will have undergone a drastic transformation. This is because our actions are no longer reactions, no longer directed pro or contra; then such "no-action" is no more a process of resistance but becomes the most positive and powerful action on earth.

But as long as you are merely seeking to become involved or as long as this is a problem to you, without going into the whole structure of our fragmentary, separate existence, your "involvement" will only represent the spiel of the ego. When there is any motivation at all, so long as there is any conscious effort to "get a piece of the action," there cannot be true involvement, since as we have seen in our inquiry the maintenance of a separate entity and such involvement are ever mutually exclusive.

Q *For many years I have been haunted by the question: "What is the purpose of Life?" I feel that unless a satisfactory answer is forthcoming, we are floundering on a sea of uncertainty. Don't you think it is for this reason, to lend some certainty and direction to our lives, that for centuries religious revelation has had such a stranglehold on the human mind? And is it not this same inherent emptiness that has driven man to carve out ever fresh goals for himself?*

A We are everlastingly asking questions—and this is a good thing, for we *must* inquire into fundamental issues—but there is an art in asking questions, the

111

right questions. The asking of a valid question already
goes a long way toward the understanding of the problem, whether the question has an answer or not. However, many of our questions are not at all legitimate
ones; that is, they make sense only *verbally,* but not
actually. To indulge in such purely intellectual activity
is to remain forever sidetracked from the real world.
When you ask, "What is the purpose of Life?" you
have already come to the conclusion that Life *has* a
purpose. How do you know? And if there *is* such a
purpose, this would imply, would it not, that there is
something over and beyond Life? If you can see
through the absurdity of such an implication, it will
become apparent that "What is the purpose of Life?"
was not a legitimate question in the first place.

We ask purposeful questions, but not very penetrating ones, because the limited consciousness of man
is essentially purposeful, and *merely* that; and it is
with the yardstick of "purpose" that we measure all
things, and we think we can also measure that which,
as Life, has brought forth all things, but which, in its
Infinity, remains itself immeasurable.

Nearly all the constructions of man, with the possible exception of his purely artistic creations, are
meant to serve some purpose; even an electronic computer producing nothing but random numbers has a
purpose—that of being totally nonpurposeful ("ran-
domness," which is ironically rather difficult to get at
on a mental level)—and so can find some use in certain statistical experiments. Since almost all our activities are utilitarian or goal-oriented, we carry over
this intensely human, deeply engrained way of think-

ing into our attitude toward the greater issues of life where, however, it is necessary to transcend our "humanity." Thus we find it difficult to view life in a non-utilitarian fashion, which is really to see things in their Suchness, to borrow a Zen expression, rather than for their potential to be what (we think) they should be. But is it not sufficient to be alive, without any thought of what purpose we fulfill? And even if individually we did fulfill a purpose in some grand scheme of things, would it *actually* make any difference to our happiness, and eliminate any suffering? Also, would it not make the individual like a pawn in some Almighty Chess Game? Is it not sufficient to do that which one loves doing—regardless of its utility or of any personal reward?

Insofar as human beings are creatures of space and time, they have this narrow teleological outlook, but to the extent that they transcend all dualistic limitations, a timeless vision is theirs. To be truly adapted to Existence, that is, to really live, we must be a kind of amphibian—equally at home in the worlds of non-duality and duality. And that becomes a possibility only through this timeless vision, which lifts us outside our petty selves. Only then shall we be able to live with the Emptiness, yet function efficiently from that Void.

Q *Why did you write in* Crisis in Consciousness *that the ending of thought is the beginning of love?*

A Love is probably the most overworked word in any language. We always talk about love, which we have classified as erotic, Platonic, profane, divine, paternal, maternal, filial, self-love, and so on, and so on. But all these categories have this in common, that they are characterized by, and dependent upon, a particular mental image; that is, they entail thought about the object of that love. Since the writer stated that Love comes with the ending of thought, he obviously could not have been referring to any of the above-mentioned types of love.

He is really trying to express something entirely different and which is also very simple, although the more we talk about it, the more complicated it seems. What he is driving at is not another, novel, category of love that nobody has yet thought about; it is not mysticism, nor is it sentimentality or what is normally understood by the term "sympathy." Essentially, it concerns setting up true relationships in one's life.

Relationship, as most of us know it, is a vicarious thing, something abstract, intellectual. I approach another human being with an idea, an image that I have about him; and he, likewise, approaches me with an image he has of me. Therefore, our relationship is vicarious, unreal; for it is only these images, which are the result of thought, of memory, that are meeting.

True relationship is possible only when the mind is empty of ideas, opinions, abstractions; that is, there is relationship, communion, only in silent observation. Such observation has no center, the observer, that weighs, compares, judges. The relationship that comes into being through observation without a center is not what is conventionally called "love," which is merely the interplay of one image with another, but a communion in which the observer, the observed, and the observation are one. Such a seeing is therefore un-warped, free from effort, free from any conflict of inter-ests, free from the wish to change the other, free from demands, free from jealousy.

Since we have created and firmly established the immutable center, the observer, with which we ap-proach every relationship, such communion is very rare in the world today. I have simply chosen to call it Love—although the word does not matter—because in such vision, in that state of experiencing and living, the world is made whole again.

12

Free
Among the
Unfree

These days there appears to be a great deal of talk in the air about freedom, which is perhaps not altogether surprising in an unfree society. A man in prison always yearns for the wide world beyond his bars. Instinctively, many of us feel that freedom is one of the greatest goods on earth, if not the greatest. But the word "freedom," like the word "love," is heavily loaded. What, actually, do we mean by it? Is it freedom of thought, or freedom from oppression, from want, from government interference? One could define many more kinds of freedom; but, however necessary all these are in a decent society, they are as nothing when set against Freedom in the most fundamental sense of the word, with which we are concerned here. This Freedom is an inner condition of mind which flourishes regardless of the outer freedom or the lack of it; at the same time it represents the only genuine way toward the achievement of the outer freedom. A free society can never come into being through the efforts of slaves, no matter what they do. And we *are* slaves, as long as we do not recognize that we are totally conditioned, that all our actions spring from the past.

Fundamentally, inner freedom is freedom from the demands of self, the self which is "you," "me," and is also the society which we have created. Since there exists no greater tyranny than that of self, the inner freedom is the ultimate freedom. But, it may be asked, how can such a thing be? How can I, being "me," be free from "me"? This seems one case where mere logic will not get us very far, because obviously our very terminology is begging the question. Since words are essential for communication, we should use them lightly, assigning only a provisional degree of finality to their meanings. In this way, we create the necessary freedom to go beyond the words, which is essential for an understanding of any depth.

Paradoxically, losing one's self is finding oneself. This means that one has to find out what one is, not in a theoretical sense—to be told one is the son of God, or made in his image, or any of that rubbish—but actually to discover for oneself what is the energy, the activity that is experienced as the "me." For the self is not to be made into an abstraction, and can therefore never be described. It is constantly in motion; it is the most evanescent thing in the world. The moment you think you know it, it is already something entirely different. As it is not within the field of knowledge, you cannot find out what that "self" is from someone else—whether he be your psychoanalyst, your favorite guru, or the present writer.

So the few words with which we can only hint at the

nature of "self-knowing" will have no meaning whatsoever, unless one is actually doing this process of self-discovery, which is meditation in the most real sense. To understand the nature of the self one must pay attention to one's actions, thoughts, and feelings; one must observe all the secret longings, quiet despairs, and inner conflicts of the mind without being carried away by what one sees. The moment one gets carried away there can be no further observation which should be as uninvolved with the scene observed as the operation of a photographic camera. If one can thus be "choicelessly aware" in watching oneself, one may find that at every moment our action is based upon a memory of a past experience; this past experience, which seeks continuation, intensification, modification, creates the future. All action is concerned with linking a present situation with a past situation, giving some continuity to that past. Therefore we never live in the present moment, although intellectually we can acknowledge that it is only the latter that exists. Is not this strange? At the same time it may be seen that we never accept what *is*, that we continually wish to mold what is into what *should be*, on the basis of past experience, conditioning. And the feeling of divergence between what is and what should be—which is really a kind of resistance against what is—is none other than the ego-sense and lies at the root of all conflict; therefore it is the only obstacle to our freedom. To be really free means that one is fully submerged in what is, no longer concerned with what is going to happen to that little self, and so no longer projects the future.

Now, when one is no longer creating time as a psychological necessity, is there then still a self? We are obviously not talking about the physical self—with its purely physical needs—but about the psychological center with its many compulsions that is the focus of all mental anguish. If that center is in abeyance, for however short a period, is there not the throwing off of a tremendous burden, and an inexpressible feeling of release? If one is free from the center, one can live totally with what *is*, without conflict, even if what *is* comprises a society of the unfree. This does not mean that one is satisfied with things as they are; or that having had a taste of total freedom, one says "I am alright, Jack" and ignores or looks down upon those who are still shackled by their desires, by their lack of comprehension of the ever restless mind. On the contrary, it means that for the first time one sees clearly the urgency of a total revolution in consciousness, without being in the least identified with its necessity. This is because there is no longer any division between oneself as a separate entity and one's fellow beings. And paradoxically, only in that state can one be truly effective in bringing about such a fundamental change in consciousness and therefore in society. Society cannot be liberated from without, by imposing on it a new set of values; its essential psychological structure is not affected by any political revolution, however drastic, or by any legislation, however humanistic. It can only be freed from within, through a complete transformation of the consciousness that underlies all that society's basic assumptions and motivations. This means that when any "individual" frees himself, in that very act he does more for the liberation of mankind than all the collective liberation movements in history. The latter's achievements are merely the pale reflections of the process of self-realization.

119

13

The Vicious,
Vicious Circle
of
Self-Defense
and War

The works of man must rest on a solid foundation to be of lasting benefit to him. This applies both individually and collectively, but if it holds true for the individuals making up a particular society, then that society will automatically be well founded. What is basically wrong with our present society is that none of its foundations are sound. That is why we shall never go very far by merely reforming it. This society holds that the means justify the end, and that might is right. For example, a so-called "just" war can insure peace. And if, until now, we have not succeeded in bringing about such a peaceful condition, it is only because we have not killed enough men—of the wrong kind, that is. If eventually a sufficient number of "wrong" ones have been eradicated, only "right" ones will remain

A Vicious, Vicious Circle....

and we shall be as good as in paradise. The only trouble with this philosophy is that different nations have somewhat mixed up the notions of "righteous" and "unrighteous," and so there will never be an end to the killing.

What then, it may be asked, are the right foundations for a society to be based upon? These foundations do not rest upon any ideology, belief, or religious revelation, which are all inspired by fear—fear by the individual to face reality, and especially the naked truth about himself. However, the right foundation is exactly that naked truth, revealed through the understanding of oneself. If one knows oneself, one will know what *is* and will be able to live with it. To know that what one is, is merely an appearance, without real substance, puts an end to the process of self-justification. There is self-justification, with its inevitable concomitants of ambition, competition, and conflict only so long as that self is taken for real. To protect that self we identify with something greater, something that appears more secure, and so create the collective aggressiveness which ever leads to wars.

One of the ways in which this aggressiveness manifests itself is through self-defense. It is easy enough to see that aggression in any form is one of the main causes of war, but many find it difficult to realize that defense equally contributes to war. And here we do not simply mean that it takes two parties to fight a battle. Since the self, psychologically, is only kept alive through continual aggressivity, self-defense is merely a continuation of that violence. Defense may be viewed as negative aggression, but none the less a form of violence. Thus wars are ever excused and given continuity by this urge for defense. What is there to defend? One's possessions, one's liberties? If one

121

feels attached to one's possessions, then one is really possessed by what one owns and therefore one has already forfeited liberty. Also, as long as we cling to our possessions we shall have fear, the fear of their loss. And fear ever engenders violence. By "possessions" we do not mean only material goods, but also ideological goods with which we are fanatically identified and for which we are even prepared to die. Thus this entire activity of self-justification as self-defense is a vicious circle which can only lead to more conflict.

So, how then is peace ever to come? It must be clear by now that peace can come only when the true meaning of "mine" and "thine" has been realized. In other words, there must be a completely different concept of self, or rather *no* concept, since in actual fact the self has merely conceptual existence; and it is this conceptual knowledge which fools everyone into accepting his self for real. The self is a relative and comparative concept. Thus, asserting one's self, by implication, means the putting down of others. Incidentally, does here not lie one of the main tasks of education, to draw attention to the necessity for self-inquiry so that all these erroneous notions may be dispelled which sour the relationships among our-"selves"?

Peace will come as soon as the individual is peaceful, no longer fosters aggression in the world through self-justification. Then, with the end of self-justification there will arise quite a different set of values. For one thing, it will spell the end of nationhood as an emotional and political hang-up. Another aspect of society that will acquire an entirely different meaning is "private property." This, also, will lose its emotional appeal for which one is willing to lay down one's life. Private property may eventually disappear, not

122

through being outlawed—which it couldn't be—but quite naturally, and without conflict, because one's possessions are no longer an extension of the self. And as to ideologies, who will need them any longer?

14

The
Only
Priority

The other day I came across an article by a distinguished biophysicist in a scientific magazine, which dealt with the present world crisis. The author had made a priority list of the major crises and problems facing humanity, arranging them according to eight different levels of urgency. He suggested that our scientific and engineering talent should be mobilized into research teams or task forces for social research and development. Then, if these groups of specialists should be able to solve the various problems, utopia could be well within our reach.

This writer regrets to say that he does not view the world's problems and their solution in such a simplistic (but essentially complicated) manner. To him, this scientist's approach is symptomatic of what ails us—the fragmented way man functions, both individually and collectively. In fact, if one had to think of one word which best characterizes the present human predicament, the term "fragmentation" may be suggested. We see this fragmentation on all levels of our existence. Inwardly, it manifests itself with the mind of man being in a continuous state of conflict—different desires pulling him in different directions—and outwardly, in practically every sphere of activity.

Sexuality provides a particularly good example of how the fragmented mind perverts and complicates something that is essentially pure, beautiful, and simple. Thus, we have divided sexual activity into various categories, such as "licit" and "illicit" sex—somewhat analogous to that other absurdity, "legitimate" and "illegitimate" children; though, for the life of me, I fail to see what all this has got to do with the law. Then, sex has become terribly involved with our strange, neurotic attitude toward nudity. Although complete nudity is our natural condition, it is under a heavy taboo in our society. This is basically because it undermines partial nakedness, which we idolize and glamorize, and which has become an indispensable element in much of our commercial art and advertising. At the same time, total nakedness is generally abhorred for several reasons. First, perhaps, it reminds us too much of our essential nakedness, since so much of our clothing represents the trappings of a socially accepted role. Secondly, we shun total nudity because "it leaves nothing to the imagination." This phrase is highly telling about our fundamentally unhealthy outlook on sex, which admits that bare sex is not enough, but that we need an additional, artificial stimulus through the imagination—which is the unreal—really to enjoy it.

Another aspect in which the fragmented mind manifests itself very clearly in the sexual area is when, instead of being attracted to another individual as a whole entity, it has a fixation on the body alone or even on particular parts of a body. Thus, it must be realized that in modern man, due to this fragmentation of thought and action—which is really intellectual specialization to the nth degree of absurdity—sex has become a thing overwhelmingly of the mind, or "intellectual," and correspondingly less the physical thing that it is supposed to epitomize. Then, to cap it all, we have separated sex from other sensuous experience and built it up to something of enormous importance; thus, it has now virtually become the sole yardstick of morality.

In the body politic we have another good example of how the fragmented mind has perverted the very purpose of politics, which is to work for the unification of mankind. Here it can be observed how politicians through their activities maintain the division of the world into separate little nationalities, all competing with one another and occasionally warring. We also see how within each nation politicians polarize the population instead of creating unison and harmony; and how they have a vested interest in maintaining the division of people as first-class and second-class citizens, as "haves" and "have-nots." We advisedly wrote "vested interest," because if there were ever to be an end to fragmentation this would spell the end of politics as we now know it. There would be no more need for rhetorics by the "leaders," no more need to play on the emotions of the "followers" and for a warped presentation of facts. What would be required then is only managers and administrators who, for a change, will be acting for *all of us*, the human race. This may entail some purely practical difficulties, like all human endeavor, but it seems to me that such worldwide planning is not beyond the ingenuity that has split the atom and landed men on the moon. Personally, I feel very strongly that where there is love there is a way; that means can be found to solve any problem, however great—something which has been proved many times over in the lives of creative individuals.

Some say man has always functioned in this inadequate, fragmented way and that it is the only kind of existence he knows; therefore he is not likely to change. Perhaps so, but as long as we are resigned to this situation we must accept the consequences and will have this world crisis in increasing severity looming over us. After all, it is we who have created this mess and we shall have to do something about it if we don't like it. Apparently we do not like it, but I doubt whether we abhor it sufficiently to take some really efficient action, so that the human species may be in command and not a conglomeration of fragments. And in this connection, the only effective action is that which springs from a total seeing, made possible when the split in the mind has been healed. This type of perception is an inherent quality of mind which comes only with total simplicity. As a child it was our essential way of functioning, but when we lost our simplicity we lost also this totality of vision. To regain it should be our first priority—this time, as mature human beings. Then we might find there are no other priorities.

15

On
Meeting
Death

How strange that it takes the loss of someone very dear to make us reflect upon the meaning of death! We talk about the "facts of life" being essential for everyone to understand, but what about the "facts of death"? To this writer, the latter are at least as important as the former; in fact, he feels that life can not really be understood properly without penetrating into the meaning of death.

Death is everywhere, and is always with us; yet, unless forcefully and painfully confronted with it, we do not wish to give the matter any thought. The reason for this—and we may not always be conscious of it—is that the fact of its existence seems to be in complete contradiction to everything we stand for. What we stand for is only too clear: more power, prestige, wealth, more experiences of every kind and intensity, and everlasting security both physical and emotional. Thus, it has become almost a necessity to surround ourselves with fantasies about Death; these somehow seem to undermine its existence and so serve to gild the lily.

When we experience a so-called "bereavement," what actually happens? The event is received with divers emotions that can add up to a traumatic experience. If the deceased occupied an important part in our life, and therefore in our thoughts, a great segment of our thought life is suddenly cut away; and it must be remembered, it is really this thought life that makes up the so-called "self." Thus, there is a great feeling of emptiness, as though a part of that self has died with the deceased. And if we are a little aware, we shall perceive how over the years we had cultivated a particular image of our self in relation to the other person; by necessity, this image has now vanished at once. Obviously, therefore, the experience gives us a foretaste of our own death, which is the complete obliteration of our thought contents, including all images of the self.

But that is not all. The death of another forcefully reminds us of our own finitude, and since we have never given the matter any deep consideration, we are never ready for death. This strengthens the ever-repressed fear of death. Finally, if all this were not bad enough, we experience the additional emotion of "guilt" when we reminisce how often we behaved beastly toward the departed. So, all these various emotions, of varying degrees of painfulness, are experienced as "suffering"; and we feel that we are rightly and inevitably suffering since under the circumstances everyone expects us to suffer—at least for a respectable period. This, of course, is one of the purposes of the mourning custom. If perchance we became a bit forgetful, and for a moment felt like acting as though it never happened, there are the decorum and paraphernalia of mourning to bring us quickly back into line. Two thousand years of Christianity have left their mark in this connection and conditioned us to worship suffering almost as an end in itself—in any case, as a virtue —and thus the austerity of the mourning period is mentally notched up as a truly virtuous act.

To the writer, there is a receptivity toward death which cannot properly be described as "suffering"; nor is it a heartless indifference. This third state of mind is singularly free of sorrow and despair; yet it is an extremely grave state of mind which ensues from being closely in touch with death —not as a concept, but as a direct experience. Because, you see, there is such a thing as experiencing death while still in the body; this means dying everyday to the petty, insignificant thought accumulations that we cherish as memories and which sustain the life of the self. But for that it is necessary to go into one's self and see that it is not the terribly important thing which you think it is. If you can do this, you will experience a tremendous surge of renewal, and of freedom. Also, you will understand that life and death form a unity, but that it is our fear which has separated them. Through fear it is impossible to come in direct contact with the thing you fear; fear always projects a concept that serves as a buffer between you and reality. Thus we have concepts about death as well as life, which prevent us from understanding either; and the fear of death casts a constant shadow over our lives.

Therefore, at least to the writer, there is an immediate inward challenge: to understand so thoroughly the meaning of death, and therefore of life, that we can cast off completely the shadow of fear. Then, when death crosses our path, there will be an entirely different experience.

130

16

Reflections on Causality: The Ultimate Failure of Metaphysics

> The insight of the inherent Emptiness of all things is the antidote to all dogmatic views; but him I declare incurable who misapprehends this Emptiness as a theory.
> Nāgārjuna

In previous writings the author has attempted to demonstrate that whenever an inquiry is pursued to its most fundamental level, certain paradoxes crop up which to all intents and purposes make nonsense of our reasoning. A case in point is the law of cause and effect—and the observation applies to both physical and psychological processes.

On the physical level, for example, it has been said by the late Professor P. W. Bridgman:

> The same situation confronts physicists everywhere; whenever he penetrates to the atomic or electronic level in his analysis, he finds things acting in a way for which he can assign no cause, for which he never can assign a cause, and for which the concept of cause has no mean-

ing, if Heisenberg's principle is right. This means nothing more nor less than that the law of cause and effect must be given up.*

In modern physics, causality has been found to be applicable only to the phenomena of the macromolecular world; on the atomic and subatomic levels, the behavior of any one particle is unpredictable. Whenever we are concerned with aggregates of large numbers of particles, these follow the laws of probability—and the superficial order which this produces in the phenomena is observed by the mind as cause and effect.

On the psychological level, in an examination of the mechanism of Memory, the author has shown elsewhere that the individual elements of memory—the memory images or "engrams"—behave equally randomly; they are acting on their own initiative, as it were. Thus, the more plausible, conventional explanation of an entity that handles these images and extracts them from cold storage in data banks is in actual fact false. In other words, the emergence of memory images—and this comprises therefore the whole process of "remembering"—is a movement without apparent cause, and so can be said to be fundamental in the true sense of the word.

These paradoxes appear to negate the concept of logical thought—that thought which presumes a causal connection between phenomena. To the present writer this conclusion does not seem warranted, but rather the paradox seems to indicate the limitations to the field of logic. The unexpected contradiction is merely a warning sign that tells the ratiocinating mind: "So far and no further—for now you are

* *Reflections of a Physicist,* Philosophical Library, New York, 1955, p. 179.

132

dealing with a fundamental state, that is, a state which itself initiates processes and events; and it is therefore unrealistic to expect a chain of cause-and-effect down the line." This situation literally defies comprehension; no amount of imagination can help us to visualize it.

A great Indian thinker, Nāgārjuna, who is believed to have lived in the second century A.D., was much perplexed by this paradoxicality. Using a strictly logical approach, he examined the concept of causality in order to find out whether it could be substantiated.* The general conclusion of his analysis was that the concept could not be proved, and that in principle there is no difference between a magical apparition and one produced in the ordinary way within a causal framework. Since cause does not give rise to the effect of itself, the two entities are really strangers and unconnected *by necessity*.

Causality, although observed with the gross senses everywhere in the world, appears to be no more than a regular association of events occurring in a certain time sequence. There is an observation that, all other circumstances remaining equal, event B always succeeds event A, but in a reasonable world we also wish to know why this should be so (that is, if there is a "why")—this is the essence of the concept of causality. The answer, however, is not forthcoming. As in all other explanations of natural phenomena, we can state "how" things work, but when asked "why" we are stumped for an answer.

Now let us explore with Nāgārjuna, and begin with the following example of his approach to the problem. First of

---

* In the *Madhyamika Karikas*: "Examination of Causality," which comprises fourteen epigrams.

all, not a thing in the phenomenal world can be said to have an absolute existence of its own (or "self-existence"), for when we describe one entity, its description and definition are always in relation, and by reference, to other entities.* It follows that if the entities are merely relative, they have no real (independent) existence. (After all, "existence" implies no qualifications; it is virtually synonymous with "independence.") Therefore, the formula, "this being, that appears" loses every meaning. We can also come to this meaninglessness by realizing that on postulating one entity, we *ipso facto* postulate also others. Why then select any one entity as the cause of a particular event?

Another aspect of causality is the following: It can be observed that there never is a single cause for an effect, but always a multiple cause. For instance, a seed does not become a sprout by itself, but needs the presence of soil, moisture, light, and so forth—in short, there are a number of causes at work to produce the effect. Now the question can be raised: If the effect is not found in the causes, either individually or collectively, how then can it logically be obtained from them? And also, how can we draw the line between causes and noncauses? Maybe there are also other, as yet unrecognized, factors indispensable to the emergence of the sprout? As Nāgārjuna put it: "Since from these causes does appear, what never existed in them, why then does it not appear from non-causes?" Also, the question arises as to what it is that coordinates all these separate factors into a (composite) cause, since such a coordinating agency becomes a logical necessity. And if there is such a coordinating

* *Cf.* the statement by Hui-neng, the founder of Chinese Zen Buddhism and the Sixth Patriarch: "From the first not a thing is."

factor, does its function not make it into a part-cause too? Then, the argument could again be applied to this extended bundle of cause-elements, in which event we quite clearly have an infinite regression on our hands.

At the moment of emergence of the sprout, the seed has already disappeared. Thus, at this instant, there is an effect without a cause. Now, how can there be any relationship between the cause and the effect when they were at no time coexistent? Relationship, by definition, requires that both entities are in existence at the same time.

Finally, the writer would like to add one more conundrum, which he feels Nāgārjuna himself might have brought up, had he been acquainted with the results of modern physics, especially quantum mechanics. If no causality is observable on the atomic level, and phenomena in the macromolecular world are derived simply by extrapolation (or building up) from that level, is it logical to posit causality on the macromolecular scale?

These points may suffice to show that the dialectical method can only lead to paradox and does not allow us to go any further in our search for clarity.

One feels it was not at all Nāgārjuna's intention to demonstrate with his analysis the impossibility of ever solving the problem of causality and to leave his readers in mid-air, as it were, but rather to show up the limitations of the discursive intellect for the task in hand. In this sense his dialectic has the same function as purported for the *koan* in Zen Buddhism: to prepare the mind for a direct understanding, which is not merely on the level of words. Moreover, he proved that in this particular instance such a limited, intellectual understanding is not even possible, since to attempt it leads only to a verbal muddle.

135

We touch here upon an interesting question of more general implication. Is understanding or "insight" to be acquired through reasoning; or is it to be attained through bypassing reason, and if so, what then is the function of reason?

This writer holds that any understanding of real depth is always instantaneous and not the result of an analytical, reasoned approach. It is a seeing in a flash, a complete perception of the truth or falseness of a proposition, however simple or however complicated; and it is only afterward that the discursive mind steps in and provides an intellectual confirmation or "proof" (thus completing the process of understanding on all levels). In this particular sequence, perception and reason are allies, but when proceeding the other way round, reason impedes (or delays) perception.

What really happens is that the rejection of the approach by the intellect is in itself the means to an understanding of that which lies beyond all words. It is not that first we reject reason and then look for another way, but in the very denial of the false approach the truth of the right approach emerges. In other words, the truth is perceived in seeing the false as the false.

There are certain people who possess this capacity of spontaneously receiving an insight into a complicated problem without going through a process of intellectual analysis. Most of us, however, are conditioned to reason things out— which is basically the technological approach—and this represents our normal response to any challenge. (Even when we react "emotionally," this is still a response essentially based upon thought, and therefore a form of mentation.) When applied to psychological problems, this approach gives a partial solution, and in this sphere anything

136

partial or fragmentary is not only inadequate but also hopelessly wrong. The very meaning of understanding is the integral act of seeing an object, a situation, or a concept from all angles, with all its relationships and all its ramifications, in one single instant.

To perceive in this fashion, the mind must be quite still, the intellect in abeyance. Do we not occasionally experience this state, as, for example, on waking up from dreamless sleep in the silence of the night, when all problems are perceived with perfect clarity? Where, however, the intellect is still active in attacking the problem, this is because it has not yet seen its irrelevance, it does not yet know its limitations and so its proper area of operation. For those who are in this condition Nāgārjuna shows all the various ways in which the analytical mind can delve into a problem, and that whatever the approach, one ends up with a paradox, a contradiction. When the mind has finally exhausted itself in this activity, it is quiet, because it has tried everything, yet got nowhere. Thus it sees its futility, and only then is it ready to let go.

Therefore, what Nāgārjuna has done is to be conceived rather as a skillful means, a pedagogic technique, than as an end in itself, the reasoning out of the mystery of causality. From within the wider context of his realization of the Emptiness of all things, he takes just one specific example and proceeds by a method, acceptable to the intellect, to demonstrate its very impotence. As another example we could mention his brilliant analysis of motion and rest, leading again to a paradox—that of the impossibility of determining either of these states. These specific cases, however, are subservient to his general thesis as to the inadequacy of all explanations: there is no proposition which cannot be

137

negated—hence the need for a Total Negation. And even from the very verbalizing of this thesis, a further paradox could be construed . . . It is for this reason that his teaching is often viewed in the West as nihilistic and self-defeating.

This opinion is due to a complete misapprehension and lack of insight in the matter. In the first place, the kind of negation we are talking about is not an annihilation; it leaves things intact on the phenomenal level, but only shows their relativity, and so their unreality. A negation which would lead to their destruction, on the other hand, would *ipso facto* admit their prior reality. Also, it must be seen that a Total Negation, which clarifies the place and role of the intellect in the scheme of things, implies an affirmation on an altogether different level, namely, of that which is nonintellectual, nondiscursive, and may perhaps be called "spiritual" (that is, if we insist on talking in terms of negation and affirmation; do we ever question their meaning and indeed the very necessity of thinking in this way?) It is greatly to the credit of Indian thinkers like Nāgārjuna and others, thousands of years ago, that already they understood that negative thinking is the highest form of thinking; whereas today, in the West, philosophers are still caught in the futile game of affirming, of searching for so-called positive values within a circle of thought and concept.

Now it seems to me that to get out of our quandary, which is to see how the paradox of causality has arisen, there is no need to study any further Nāgārjuna's fourteen verses in a process of thesis-antithesis-synthesis. We shall immediately go to the heart of the matter if we can penetrate into the meaning of the elements upon which his analysis was based: identity, difference, existence, and nonexistence.

First then we must see that Reality, the World, is inherently not determinate, not tangible, and not divisible or classifiable, but appears to be all these things through the activity of the brain. Owing to its neurophysiological make-up, this human computer with its extensions, the sense organs, can handle only discrete "bits" of information: it perceives the world as separate entities—as "things," "events," and "ideas"—and the correlation of these entities is what we call "thinking."

In its most primitive form this thinking, owing to the inherently digital nature of the cognitive mechanism, deals with the entities within a binary scale: first by affirmation and negation (such as yes-no, existence-nonexistence, and in the computer, 1–0) and once affirmed, by comparison: identity-nonidentity. These then are the basic elements of the brain's thought-patterns. Normally, when we try to "understand," "explain," or "visualize" a problem, it is no more than an exercise in fitting the entities into a particular pattern, a frame of reference, with which we are familiar—in other words, our conditioning.

In this way, thought has created the division of Reality into "things" and "events," into "past," "present," and "future," into "cause" and "effect"—and now this same thought is trying to "understand" why this division exists. But is such a thing at all possible? Is it not like putting on dark glasses and asking why the world looks so dark? Nowhere does one find a highly ingrained sense of "time" that is capable of utilizing "cause and effect" for its own ends, except in association with a brain that has attained an advanced stage on the evolutionary scale.

Having come thus far in our inquiry, the situation looks really quite interesting. Because now the question must

139

logically present itself: Is the mind, or Consciousness, to be equated with the computer mechanism of the brain, with its inherent limitations, or is it that, but also something much more? Thus, the materialist—who views Consciousness as a mere by-product of the brain, analogous to the secretion of bile from the liver—is faced with a further paradox: "If the brain creates the world, what then creates the brain?"

17

The
Free
Mind

> This world is by nature composed of disjointed parts. It is held together by cause and effect like loose sand by a clenched fist.
>
> Aśvaghosha

Some time ago an anguished letter appeared in the correspondence columns of the London *Daily Telegraph,* in which the writer was much perturbed by the fact that somebody had accurately foretold the outcome of a number of matches in a recent football World Cup Final. The clairvoyant concerned had afforded indisputable proof of his prediction by depositing before the event the results inside a sealed envelope with a disinterested party. This true prognostication, our correspondent maintained, necessitated a revolution in his outlook on life which he found it extremely painful to make. What worried him particularly was that his cherished notions of virtue and sin now had to go by the board. For how could there be such things at all, if everything was predetermined and therefore one's choice be-

141

tween "good" and "evil" was also foreordained? Would this not make a mockery of the whole concept of personal responsibility?

In the preceding chapter of this book we began to look into the matter of causality and discovered an aspect of it that might be described as puzzling, like any paradox which is not immediately understood in its origin. But however interesting that aspect in itself may be, we did not on that occasion touch upon the really vital issue, the problem of Freedom and its evident negation by causality—rightly perceived by our newspaper correspondent as an extremely disturbing question even if for the wrong reasons—which alone is of the utmost importance.

In trying to resolve this predicament many thinkers, especially in the West, have looked for a kind of compromise and sought to reconcile free will with precognition, without however squarely facing the inherent contradiction which such a reconciliation would entail. One way of explaining (away) this contradiction has been to suggest that what is foreseen is merely a trend, a possibility, but not the actual event itself; and that the individual still has room left for manoeuvre, either in acceding with or in eluding the trend. This, of course, leaves free will intact but, it seems to me, does not hold water in the following specific cases: where the event is highly improbable, the odds against its happening being of astronomical magnitude; and where the prognosticator provides a large number of, perhaps irrelevant, details which are subsequently verified. Both these eventualities point to the *event* having been foreseen, not a mere trend.

Generally speaking, the conclusion is shirked that precognition implies an ineluctable determinism. To this purpose

142

some commentators even adduce the paradox implied in causality which we discussed in the previous chapter. They argue that since events merely follow one another in a regular sequence but without apparent inner necessity, freedom is not invalidated.*

As usual in controversial issues of this kind, to refer to authorities or to text-books of philosophy is not going to be of much help, and we might end up even more confused about the matter than when we started. There seems no other way out than to attempt discovering for ourselves where the truth lies. So let me try to summarize in the simplest terms what the issue is about and why, in the writer's opinion, it holds a problem that is crying out for a solution. Observation tells us that everything in the world is subject to the law of cause and effect and is therefore a function of the past; in other words, the rule of determinism appears to be firmly established. Since we ourselves form part of this world, we are in no way exempt from this law. Therefore, everything that we are today is only the result of past forces and conditions; and similarly, what we shall be tomorrow or in ten years' time is already decided by what we are today.

Are we then mere automatons, victims of circumstances beyond our control, and so doomed to live forever in sorrow and confusion? Or, notwithstanding all appearances to the contrary, is there yet a way of life which is not "fated," not mechanical, not meaningless, but creative from moment to moment, thereby cutting us free from such incidentals as birth and upbringing?

* For a typical example of this reasoning, see the article on "Free will and precognition" in Chambers's Encyclopaedia, 1959. London (George Newnes Ltd.), Vol. 11, p. 169.

Far-reaching Implications

The writer feels it is imperative to find the right answer to this question; to him it presents a direct challenge and he has therefore made it his personal problem, although it really is—or should be—everyone's problem, the concern of mankind. On its outcome must depend one's whole attitude to life. For if the mind is exclusively a mechanical entity, and therefore all thoughts, actions, and feelings flowing from it are determined, then nothing can be done and nothing matters anymore.

In that case I would be like a swimmer caught in a powerful current, completely helpless to control my course. However hard I struggle and thrash my arms and legs about through the water, my body is swept away relentlessly. Similarly, whatever I am trying to do about my destiny is useless, because the effort, too, is part of this very same destiny; and my freedom of action is illusory, being merely relative to myself when that very self is not even free, but is controlled by superior forces of which it is unconscious.

If the mind is of this nature, it also follows that there is only one fate for Man, both collectively and individually—a fate which results from events in the dimmest past of the human race. Then a spiritual life becomes an impossibility and an irrelevance, for that life implies first and foremost the freedom to be an individual rather than an entity fortuitously shaped and molded by the forces of the past. Then also the religious mind can only be a case of gross self-deception, and there is absolutely no place in one's life for meditation. Nor is there any point in a search for the Ultimate, if we are to be forever constrained within the bounds of time and space.

144

But, on the other hand, if my original premise were to prove wrong, and the mind is inherently free, but due to its ignorance, its conditioning, allows itself to be tethered by cause and effect, there may be a possibility of functioning in an entirely different manner—in such a way that it is a joy to be alive. Then, in order to come across that state, the all-important question must be: "How shall we live?"

How Do We Approach the Problem?

In the previous chapter it was suggested that there are two fundamentally different approaches to the kind of issue under discussion. Either we try to reason things out, intellectually, by applying deduction and induction, using any experimental evidence that is available; or we see through the crux of the problem immediately and only afterward fill it out with intellectual analysis, perhaps providing some sort of "proof." It was pointed out on that occasion that it is only the second of these possible approaches that can be really fruitful where it concerns solving psychological problems.* The present topic is a case in point, but for the time

---

* Even on the scientific level this approach operates to a greater extent than is realized by nonscientists. It is generally assumed that a scientific theory or hypothesis is derived entirely by a process of induction from a number of established facts. Yet it happens only too often that an hypothesis is conceived, in a flash as it were, without too much regard for the experimental evidence or the lack of it. So, instead of thinking from the particular to the general, the scientist has arrived at this latter stage immediately by his direct vision of nature's operating mechanism. This vision leaves no room for alternative hypotheses which in theory would explain the facts equally well, and is subsequently confirmed by fresh evidence.

As examples of this intuitive, nondiscursive approach in science one might adduce the following: Kekulé's discovery of the chemical structure of benzene; Darwin's theory of evolution; and the hunch that led Madame

145

being we must proceed cautiously, step by step, since there are several issues entangled with one another which have to be unraveled first before there can be any possibility of clarification.

Relevance of Experimental Evidence

First of all, there is the evidence of precognition which appears to support determinism. It is not my present task to weigh this evidence, but for the purpose of the investigation I shall assume it to be acceptable. To the aforementioned letter writer, although the free will–determinism* controversy has been going on for centuries, it is this evidence which finally settled the argument. Now, unfortunately or fortunately, I am not qualified to comment upon such theological concepts as "virtue" and "sin," being singularly ignorant in these matters; but for the life of me I cannot see why the evidence has come as such a shock to our correspondent. Does it, in fact, mean anything new? Has not determinism always been the only mechanism we know? Are not all those phenomena deterministic which are susceptible to scientific analysis and measurement? And since we no longer believe in magic (or do we?), is it not im-

---

Curie to her discovery of radium (possibly also Einstein's theory of relativity?). On this interesting subject see further Dr. Ian Morris's article: "Is Science Really Scientific?" in the December 1966 issue of *Science Journal*, Iliffe Associated Press, London.

* From now on I propose to drop the term "free will," since these very words constitute a hindrance to understanding and, in a way, beg the question. Can will ever be free? Is not will desire in action, and so the very expression of causality on the psychological level? Fundamentally, "free will" is a contradiction in terms; it would therefore be far better to speak of the "freedom-determinism" controversy.

plicitly assumed that all manifested phenomena, on whatever level, are amenable to such treatment? It seems to me that even the word "determine" gives us a clue here, having the double meaning of "ascertain," "measure," and "fix," "decide the future."

An additional complication regarding the evidence is that even if we accept that all physical events are determinate, this is not really the issue at all. The question in dispute is the freedom of the mind—that is, whether psychological phenomena are deterministic, and whether they necessarily always are. A correct forecast of a natural disaster, such as an earthquake, would obviously not disprove freedom of mind. On the other hand, a true forecast of a mental state would afford proof of determinism on the psychological level, but only in that particular case. It would not prove that freedom is impossible to realize, or that there is no such state. By the nature of things, any evidence based on precognition can only be negative; it may prove determinism in a particular case, but will never be able to demonstrate either the possibility or impossibility of the mind being free from Time. A liberated person is beyond any degree of predictability and, paradoxically, his state must therefore be beyond every form of proof. For these reasons, we shall drop the matter of evidence as of no further concern.

Investigation of the Term "Indeterminate"

Having disposed of what now appears to be a side issue, I would like to simplify matters yet further by looking into the basic meaning of the term "indeterminate," which might

147

well give rise to some confusion. To a certain extent it really is a question of semantics. When we say, "The future is indeterminate," what exactly do we mean by "indeterminate"—and more particularly, to whom? What is indeterminate to the person with a slide rule may become predictable, and so determinate, for the man armed with a computer, or simply, with more knowledge. Perhaps some confusion exists between the notion of indeterminate as "impossible or highly difficult to predict" and that of "the future is completely open," where the latter denies that any causal connection between events exists at all.

Let me illustrate this further. I once had a lawyer friend —a very sharp thinker in his field—who for many years had meditated upon the problem of the criminal mind and was thus inevitably driven to consider such concepts as "individual responsibility" and "freedom." His observation of human behavior had led him to the pessimistic conclusion that human nature is immutable, and that in fact we are not free agents. His "solution"—if one may call it that—to make life indeterminate was to bypass personal choice in every act of decision-making by evoking chance. Only thus, he argued, could man live in freedom—by subjecting every prospective action to the tossing of a coin or the throwing of dice.

My friend was quite obviously confused between, on the one hand, that which is not easily amenable to analysis and so to prediction, and on the other hand, a suspension of the law of cause and effect. For why should the tossing of a coin be considered as indeterminate? I may not be able to predict its outcome, not having all the relevant data, but that does not entitle me to state that the event is indeterminate, being altogether beyond causation. The very fact that such an event as the tossing of a coin obeys the law of probability actually confirms its determinate nature: if we had a "perfect" coin all determining causes leading to a "head" would balance all causes leading to a "tail," resulting in approximately equal numbers of heads and tails.

There is a further factor which detracts from making the coin tossing type of experiment for decision-making a truly indeterminate event, namely the form in which the problem is presented to the tool of pure chance, or one might say the way our gambling apparatus is being "programmed." The totality of potential action conceivable by the mind has to be split into a number of well-defined courses, one of which is to be selected by chance, subsequently to be enacted. But this act of presentation is still man-made and contains therefore in itself the proclivities of a particular mind, thus introducing a deterministic factor. The difficulty of its elimination is somewhat analogous to that of finding out the truth of an issue by submitting it to a debating society, where the very formulation of the motion up for debate, requiring only a yes or no type of answer, is already a violation (that is, a limitation) of the truth. This is hardly surprising considering that the whole concern of the debate is the winning of an argument and not establishing the truth of any matter.

Resolution of the Semantic Difficulty

Recapitulating our discussion so far, we have seen that the problem, when tackled on the lines of my lawyer friend, becomes one of immense difficulty, if it is considered in isolation—as a specialized case—because it invariably in-

The Free Mind

volves the question of the "knower." The idea of being indeterminate—merely in the sense of being difficult to predict—must of necessity be associated with the "knower," who can or cannot determine or "read" a particular causal relationship. And it is always possible to imagine a knower whose knowledge is so great that to him even the most intractable, the most indeterminate, becomes determinate.

Thus, for the purpose of this investigation, "indeterminate" as defined in the previous paragraph means "determinate," since it admits of the law of cause and effect. Also, in this connection, an experiment such as decision-making by coin tossing is seen to be a red herring and can be dismissed for the purpose of this inquiry.

What Are the Known Facts?

Having somewhat split up the various issues involved in this complex problem, it is perhaps easier at this stage to ascertain the relevant facts. First of all, as we have seen in the beginning of this chapter, at least on the material level the rule of determinism is firmly established; and this I feel has never been seriously doubted. In the previous chapter we mentioned that the only exceptions to causality are those events that can be said to be "fundamental." Although this is largely a matter of definition, the fact is, however, that certain phenomena in nature (mainly those connected with fundamental particles) do not seem to come within the law of cause and effect (Heisenberg's Uncertainty Principle!); we may therefore say that they are "self-caused."

Secondly, on the psychological level, I have no reason

to doubt that the mind, as we normally see it function, is equally subject to causality. I only have to look around me, and within, to know that men without exception are driven along by their desires, whether they are conscious of them or not. We see this fact at its most dramatic in the lives of the so-called great men of history, the "men of destiny," who pursued their goals with an iron will, making everything else subservient to the continuity of an idea. Here, we see with great perspicuity the unfolding of the destiny by which these individuals were being carried along; and how, being unconscious of the dynamics involved, they never had a real chance to extricate themselves from their fates. However, because these cases are so spectacular in comparison with our own humdrum lives, we should not deceive ourselves that fundamentally we are placed differently.

Now the task I have set myself is to find out whether determinism must ever be an inescapable fact, or whether —analogously to what, as we have discovered, applies on the material level—there are certain exceptions also on the psychological level. In other words, I ask myself whether it is possible for the mind to function in such a way that its every moment, every action, represents a fundamental event, that is, an event totally divorced from the past which molds the present. If this were possible—and I have a hunch it is, for on the most fundamental level of reality there is probably no longer a division between "physical" and "psychological" events—then such a mind would function in absolute freedom, without needing recourse to the paraphernalia of games of chance!

In order to investigate this possibility, I propose to look somewhat more closely into the mechanism whereby the mind is held within the bonds of causality; moreover, I think this is the only feasible method. Having penetrated to what is probably the heart of the matter, I feel I may henceforth allow some more scope to the approach of directly seeing psychological facts, and correspondingly less to the discursive treatment.

The Importance of Being Indeterminate

If there are still those who think that the question of Freedom is a rather academic one that does not really affect them, I would like to point out how it directly impinges on our state of living continually with conflict, which is a necessary result of causality. So unless one is resigned to this life, with its never-ending sorrow and utter meaninglessness, the issue becomes of vital importance.

Looking at the basic conflict situation in the mind, and expressing this in its simplest form, it can be said there is a progression of torturing thoughts; and the ironical part is that we cannot do a thing about it. This in itself should be a sufficiently strong indication for those who will not accept, who do not yet see, that man's freedom is illusory and that his fate is determinate, much like the groove of a gramophone record. For, as we have seen elsewhere, these thoughts—*any* thoughts—are completely outside our control; they appear and disappear on their own initiatives, apparently according to a law which we do not understand. Contrary to what is commonly believed, the "I" cannot manipulate the fleeting thoughts, but these thoughts manipulate the "I"; or to put it slightly differently, when we are under the impression that we are thinking, we are really "being thought." Although superficially it seems possible to "repress" a tormenting thought, the "repressing" thought is subject to the same law; it is spawned by thought itself and will only add to the turmoil. And that which has been overcome once has to be overcome again and again.

This is the first thing we will have to learn: that the more we interfere with thought, the more we shall get entangled with it, and the more thought will persist—truly a vicious circle. As little as we can stop dreams troubling our sleep can we bring the stream of disturbing thoughts to an end. So where then is our much-vaunted freedom?

Facing all these facts, and realizing in particular our utter helplessness, we may resign ourselves to the situation and continue to live in a cage of the past. Perhaps, then, we become followers of some existentialist philosophy of despair, or adhere to some such slogan as "Live only for the present," as though this would make the slightest difference to our plight.

But have we not overlooked something? Beyond the fact that thought is evidently autonomous, that the ego cannot control the contradictory thoughts—and if it could, there would obviously be no conflict in the mind—but is controlled by them, what do we actually know of thought? For instance, why does a particular thought arise? Perhaps if I can understand the law which governs its emergence (if there be such a law), I may be able to discover a state in which thought no longer automatically arises, because the basic conditions responsible for its emergence have changed or are no longer present. This would place the mind at once beyond the process of causality, free it from contradiction and enable the brain to experience a moment —or period—of complete stillness, and so clarity. By this

153

we do not mean that the mind goes blank, or falls asleep, but that thoughts are no longer compelled by the need for ego-building and sustenance which is responsible for spinning the thread of our "destiny."

Although I can see quite clearly that it is impossible for me to do anything to bring about this state in a positive way—for this would only lead to backing up thought— may it not be possible to do so in a negative way, that is, indirectly?

Determinism Represents Repetition and Limitation

The iron hand of causality rules everywhere in the known world and, it is assumed by most scientists, everywhere in the universe. On the material level it characterizes the repetitive, inflexible nature of phenomena. For example, every time I bring sodium and water in contact with each other, an explosive reaction follows. This repetitiveness applies also to the sphere of living things: an acorn, if it develops at all, will always grow into an oak and not, say, into an elm; a tadpole is ever to become a frog, and so on— illustrating the determinism of conditioned origination. Therefore, causality obviously represents limitation, specialization, which is the very essence of determinism. But going one step further, we see all this occurring also on the psychological plane, within the type of consciousness we know: because the mind always revolves around its past experiences, all so-called new experience is in essence a mere repetition of an old experience with some modifications, the reappearance of an old pattern of thought and action. Thus, all we know and will ever know is a continuity of the old, that is, a variation on the known; and the Un-known is forever to remain just that.

Without causality—the bond of time—all this would not and could not be. It is therefore true to say that Aś-vaghosha's "clenched fist" (quoted at the head of this chapter) not only holds the disjointed parts of nature together, but also has set the universe in motion. Perhaps it would be more accurate to say that it *keeps* the universe moving, after the "parts" have come into being (that is, if they have not always been there, for to talk of creation is already speculation). At present, science cannot tell us much more about the basic principle that controls the physical universe (assuming such a principle exists). Maybe it is to be equated with the force of gravity (about whose nature very little is known yet), with some unified electromagnetic field such as had been Einstein's vision; or perhaps its secret is to be found within the nature of space-time itself.

Desire—the Mainspring of Cause-and-Effect in the Psyche

However interesting these scientific problems may be, our main concern in this inquiry is the realm of the psyche, and here the leading question is: What is the working principle behind the "clenched fist" which by imposition of the tyrannical rule of causality restrains the mind, pre-vents it from attaining its freedom? Has not Aśvaghosha very appropriately used the symbol for "grasping" in his analogy, and so given us a clue? Is it not grasping—that is, desire not understood—which binds us to the past, keeps us

155

unaware of the totality of life, so that each action which the mind sponsors is incomplete, wishing to complete itself in further action?

A total action never leaves a trace; but an incomplete action, springing from an unfulfilled desire, from a thought not completely digested, ever leads to more thought, to a repetition of the experience, to further "busyness"—the urge to find fulfillment at some future time. An unresolved problem recurs again and again as thought, thus giving continuity to the mind's agitation. So basically the trouble lies in our lack of awareness, in not going to the full depth of experience, in our superficial and shallow living—in our abysmal ignorance of the basic thought processes that drive us and "give direction" to (that is, determine) our lives.

Thus the mind is forever mulling over the past, without however being able to dissolve it. At the same time, owing to this continuity of thought, there never is a possibility of perceiving the present untainted by the past. Our situation is that to every challenge we respond from the background of experience, our conditioning, which thus becomes the limiting factor in our dealings with life. Every inadequate response then leaves a further residue around which thought crystallizes, and so on, in an endless progression. Just as on the biological level it is Memory in a general sense (through the mechanism of the genes) that is responsible for the very specialized development noticeable in the reproduction of the species as well as the individual, so it is psychological memory which is the culprit in both collective and individual consciousness for narrowing down the field of the mind, creating its frontiers, and tethering the mind to what has already been.

Our meditation should be concerned first and foremost

156

with knowing and understanding—and thereby removing
—the hindrances, the mental blockages, that stand in the
way of a timeless vision. Such vision is essential, for it is this
alone that makes possible an action that is complete, that
constitutes an adequate response to the challenge of the
moment. To inquire into these matters, therefore, involves
the unraveling of the mechanism of suffering rather than a
search for the Unknown. Only in becoming aware of the
handicaps that the mind has voluntarily and unknowingly
accepted, shall we begin to look in the right direction for
our freedom. So our first task must be to investigate in
greater detail how grasping brings into being causality,
thereby reducing the mind to the level of a computer, a
clever robot.

Analogy Illustrating
the Subjection of Thought to Causation

Most readers will probably know that in physics and
mathematics a point in space is located by its coordinates
in reference to a system of three mutually perpendicular
axes or surfaces which intersect in one point of origin; that
is, the position of the first point is completely determined,
fixed, by three numbers representing the distances to each
of the reference planes. The coordinate system may have
been erected entirely arbitrarily, or perhaps with mathematical convenience in mind; it may have been anchored
to the earth or to the solar system in a certain orientation.
Whatever may be the case, the essential thing here is that,
by virtue of making it serve as a reference base, we have
endowed the system with some kind of absoluteness which

in reality it does not possess. Consequently, this quality of absoluteness is conveyed also to the point in question. (It was only with the advent of Einstein's theory of Special Relativity that scientists began to realize there is no such thing as an absolute frame of reference in which to pin down phenomena in the physical universe.)

Now, it seems to me that when we come to examine how a particular thought is related to associated thoughts and to time, the simple geometrical reference system described above may in several ways act as a helpful analogy. Consciousness may be visualized as an ever-expanding, three-dimensional network, the strands of which are made up of thoughts flowing into one another by association. A thought in the present is surrounded by associated thought and patterns of thought, all of the past, from which it has sprung.

Any thought (like the geometrical point) has reality only insofar as it relates to its matrix; but the same also applies to the matrix, which itself is the result of earlier conceptual patterns, and so on—in a regression through time to the earliest imprint, the primeval conditioning, in man's consciousness. Just as a point in space, unrelated to any other geometrical entities, has no mathematical significance, so a particular thought on its own, out of the context of social thinking, isolated from the network of thought, has no meaning; it is merely a link in the chain of determinants enforcing causality in the psyche. From this it also follows that thought can never produce a single statement that formulates the whole truth, such statement always needing further qualification. The truth can therefore never be verbalized, presented piecemeal, as an abstraction (words are thoughts, concepts, symbolized for convenient communication—and the word is therefore not the "thing"); and it can be visualized only when there is a vision of totality in which the particular is viewed from the universal (the latter representing the frame of reference, capable of infinite expansion) and not vice versa. It may be noted how we have arrived at the same insight as that expressed in Nāgārjuna's paradox in the dialectic of his Madhyamika, namely, that any statement, however profound, can be controverted and that the truth can only emerge from a process of continual and total negation. (Readers who wish to pursue the latter aspect further are referred to Nāgārjuna's teaching of *Sunyata,* the Void, already briefly discussed in our previous chapter.)

Formation of the Ego

With the thought-structure as described above originates the concept of our separateness: first physically and then ensuing from it through a process of identification, also psychologically. This psychological space-time world view constituting the ego is kept alive and strengthened by a continual crystallization of thought patterns as memory, containing all the experiences—from the most frustrating to the most gratifying, the many insults as well as the many flatteries—which have left a mark on the mind and represent the total impact of the "outside world" on our self-projected separateness. Since it is thought that has created the "I," it is only thought that can defend the artificial entity (or, so thought purports) against the onslaught of the facts that deny, that ignore the life of the ego. Contrary to what is widely held, there is ever a large—and unbridge-

159

able—gap between thought and fact; there is no such thing as "objective thought." Thought can never come to terms with the fact, the present, since on account of its inherent nature (which is grounded in Memory, the past) it is always leaning on the past, on other thought equally subjective. Yet despite this lack of solid basis, we trust entirely to thought, which to us is terribly important: we hold opinions, have views and beliefs, with a fixed determination as though we were dealing with facts. As long as we are doing this, we are out of touch with Life—for thought is not only different from the fact, but it will always prevent us from coming into contact with that fact. For example, if I am jealous, and keep thinking about it—explain away, rationalize, suppress, or feel guilty—I shall never know, never come face to face with, and so learn about, myself.

To take a view, a position, as the result of an experience ill understood, rents the mental universe asunder. This may sound dramatic, but it signifies that the mind sets up discrimination: it singles out certain experiences which it has had and identifies itself with these, all this activity being based upon pleasure.* Consequently, there is the endeavor to interfere with any facts impinging on the objects of identification; and at once thought jumps to life in this action, for thought *is* really the interference. Thus a

---

* The Third Zen Patriarch, Seng-ts'an, characterized this situation as follows:

> "A split hair's difference,
> And heaven and earth are set apart!
> If you wish to perceive that which is true
> Have no fixed thoughts either for or against it."

He also stated that to cling to likes and dislikes is the very disease of the mind.

160

fixation is set up within a frame of reference—the ending of innocence. It is the first step in seeing that which is relative, arbitrary, empty, as absolute, indeterminate, substantial—and so the first illusion from which all ignorance springs. Henceforth, all one's thinking is from a fixed point.

Realization of Our Being

Every thought is engendered and determined within a framework of thought-constructs, both collective and individual (but it is also thought that is making the distinction between the latter). If we are a little observant, we shall be able to prove this to ourselves and see that any thought occurring in the present is only a repetition, a continuation of previous thought activity; and we shall also perceive how the thought fits into an ideational pattern of the past, of our experience, our established outlook on life. Because the mind is forever in this state of recognition, it never lives wholly in the present. No new fact is ever observed as standing on its own, afresh, when the observation would be made and forgotten, but it is immediately referred back to, and viewed in the light of, the reference system of the "I," giving new life to that "I." Hence any new experience is only partially understood (total understanding can only be outside any reference system)—understood from a particular point of view only. This leaves a residue, a quantum of "conditioning," which is filed away, fitted into the self's frame of reference. Thus comes into being the ever-increasing network of thought, of knowledge with purely psychological bearing, which is the burden we carry with us in memory.

161

Let me put this in different words, for further clarification. Essentially, our life is based on certain silent assumptions about what our condition should be, and when reality clashes with expectations we suffer—there is bitterness. Do not say, "but others' expectations are fulfilled, they are luckier." In the first place, what do we really know about others? Secondly, but more fundamentally, such fulfillment, if any, only nourishes the ego and therefore maintains a state of reliance on externals. And there can be no release in that state, which implies comparative thinking and, therefore, envy and also being hooked by the psychological structure of society. And as long as there is psychological dependence, there can be no true happiness.

The ego, or state of duality—call it whatever you like—has come into being only with these unspoken assumptions, with the creation of a particular center, a limited viewpoint, upon which our thinking, our whole outlook on life, hinges. The creation of this center has come about—and we re-create it with our every thought, every experience—as an escape, a flight from the Void, the Nothingness which we are.

It is through these complicated and subtle processes that thought, although it has the illusory quality of standing on its own, of "absoluteness," is always dependent upon past activity, and in this it not only obeys the law of causality but is the very medium by and in which causality is enacted. Strictly speaking, therefore, we are not individuals, because the mind is not truly independent; and the patterns of thought that shape our individualities, which we think are uniquely our own, are derived from the patterns of collective consciousness. Understanding the origin of individual consciousness, we see this as an abstraction, a narrowing down from within collective consciousness.

Just as the point in space is given some semblance of absolute reality by the frame of reference within which it is suspended—without this coordinate system it would be completely indeterminate—so each thought is given the appearance of reality by the supporting network of thought-constructs—experience, attitudes, and "knowledge"—within which it was erected. Resulting entirely from this existing structure, every new thought and experience is completely determinate.

And again, as with our point in space, if we take away the referents—that is, question the validity of the old that has produced the present—the whole structure collapses: we are completely insecure, but also the mind is outside space and time!

To expose this network of thought patterns, and wipe it away completely, all the bonds that tie us to the past and together constitute the past—the *only* past—is meditation, a great unburdening and cleansing of the mind. But this network must be tackled in its totality. To stop anywhere abruptly is not meditation but introspection or psycho-analysis. Then we are still caught within thought; it leaves the past intact, and does not bring into being Freedom.

Not to stand in reference to any thing (psychologically) means to be nothing, to be completely transparent. Then the thought in the present, when and if it occurs, is seen to be totally transient and is robbed of its time-binding power; that is, it stops at that and no longer gives rise to further thought which compels us in one direction or another. There is no more commitment: the chain of cause-and-effects is broken! A transformation has taken place: the mind is for the first time truly independent, no longer part

163

of the Collective, and as a result, truly unique. It is unlike anything that has been known, that can be analyzed, and that can be recognized. Such a mind lives in eternal spring-time, renewing itself at each moment of its existence.

Man—the Image Maker

Whereas physically my being a separate entity is only too obvious, psychologically there is only the idea, the picture I have of myself as somebody and which I carry with me in memory. This feeling of being an ego results from identification of thought with form (that is, the body) and comprises the manifold roles that Society has imposed on me and that I have accepted. It is really quite a complex thing, resulting from the interaction of a number of thought streams: what I think of myself (that is, how I view my various accumulations, both material and psychological), what I like to think of myself, but also what I think others think of me, and what I would like others to think of me— all these conceptual strands make up the individual's refer-ence system, his orientation in Society, his very "I." Hence we can understand the ego's unenlightened interest in public opinion; for the "I," although made up of dead memory images, is deceptively like a living thing. It is never content to be itself, but is all the time adjusting to reactions and interaction with the outside world—especially with other ideational, insecure egos—in order to protect and embellish its image. As long as I play this game, consciously or unconsciously, I have—or rather, I am—this composite picture, which is all the time comparing, demanding, push-ing, guiding all my actions, and so is creating continuity.

Why have we created these pictures of ourselves in the first place and why do we maintain them? Obviously, because it gives us pleasure and provides us with (a feeling of) psychological security; it covers our inward poverty and enables us to go forward in thoughtlessness, never questioning any fundamental issues. Man is forever in search of an identity, which is to be safely anchored within some frame of reference; without it life would be completely uncertain and therefore, we think, unbearable. Fear comes into being when the possibility is glimpsed of being stripped of this identity by whatever causes, and of losing the last bulwark—which would be experienced as a kind of dying. The identity need not necessarily be restricted to one's own narrow self; the secure reference system may equally well be expansive, erected by identification with another's image—for instance, the father fulfilling himself in his son—or by identification with an ideal or an "ism."

Understanding this activity of the mind which continually prevents man from being in touch with Reality explains also his poverty of relationship, and his feeling of inward isolation. This isolation is due to the fact that we never really meet. As we have seen, each of us carries a picture of some sort with him, and what we call human relationship is only the interaction of these images which are abstractions of the real, living persons. For example, when we inquire about a stranger, generally the first thing we want to know is what are his antecedents; that is, we wish to have sufficient data at our disposal to place him in a familiar frame of reference, so that we can cope with the unknown. Since the ego is founded only on transient thought, it is ever striving to find inward security, that is, illusory strength in the form of self-boosting ideation, from its interaction with other human beings. That is why such relationships are really subtle forms of exploitation and can never lead to freedom from causality, in which is implied the very opposite: the destruction of the continuity in memory of the ego image.

Snapping the Chain of Causality: Meditation

At present our relationships with things and ideas as well as people are but the crystallized residues of thoughts, experiences, and habitual attitudes; they all go to make up the network of thought that inevitably leads to the creation of a particular reference system, the ego. The rigidity implied in the structure of the reference system, this mass of crystallized thought, can be considered as the expression of the Law of Inertia on the psychological level. The resolving of this whole structure, which implies the wiping away of any reference system, is what Krishnamurti often speaks of as the dying at every moment to everyone of our relationships. Then one stands completely alone, but not in the sense of being lonely, cut off from all relationship. On the contrary, it means to be related to everything, yet not dependent upon, not involved with, and not influenced by, a single thing.

To be out of any reference system, to be totally innocent of any picture, any identity, is like being a stranger to oneself. This, I feel, is how life should be met if one wishes to live totally in the present moment and so out of the clutches of time, causality, sorrow. Sorrow is then powerless to assail us, for there is only the fact and no thought trying to intervene with it; and is it not thinking about the fact—

166

rather than the fact itself—that is the sole cause of our unhappy state?

When we realize that all our cherished aspirations and ideals that mold our entire existence are but inventions of the mind, the results of idea, then the events in our life are truly like visions in a dream. After all, is there anything more transient than thought, although mere repetition may lend it some (apparent) continuity and substance?

To liberate thought from the past, to destroy its absoluteness and reveal its relativity, its dependence upon concepts and ideas, equally relative and arbitrary, is true meditation. But this has to be a total process; it must strike at the very roots of each thought to be effective.

What usually passes for meditation is only introspection; and psychoanalysis is a particular form of introspection. What these processes do is to reveal a certain neglected area of our mental life—much that is hidden, murky, that we do not wish to face, since it is riddled with contradiction and in conflict with social attitudes and edicts. Starting with the thought occurring in the present, some of the thought patterns immediately associated with it are exposed to the focus of consciousness and so, to a certain extent, understood. But this is still a partial process, essentially a concentration of the attention. For example, an "inferiority complex" is shown to exist, and so an immediate conflict situation is perhaps wiped out. But a much deeper, more fundamental, conflict situation—inherent in our very thinking in terms of "superior" and "inferior"—remains untouched.

Similarly, a sick man is preferably not confronted, or does not confront himself, with the fact of death; therefore he is never free from fear. The thoughts and concepts that are left untouched are always those which are inextricably interwoven with the final self-assertion and preservation of an individual, that is, his maintenance as a separate entity. To take these away is literally and figuratively "unthinkable" to an ego that has not yet come to terms with Death. For the truth is that without these basic supporting and comforting concepts and thought patterns that form the very fringes of the web of thought making up individual consciousness, there would be no separate entity whatsoever. To touch the most eschewed nooks and corners of the mind it is necessary to question all our silent assumptions about thought, about our motives and our most basic attitudes to life. This necessarily involves examining the standards of society, to which we at present adhere to a greater or lesser extent, and knowing all the underlying concepts of collective consciousness which are not only never challenged but of which we are totally unconscious.

So meditation is proceeding from one thought, and reducing all thought connected with the first to nothingness: to see all the patterns, the immediate as well as the ultimate ones, as concerned with the assertion of I-ness. This, I feel, is what Krishnamurti means by "thinking out, feeling out a thought to its very end."

The reason why so often we stop short in our meditation is that we dare not face the ultimate motives of our action; and we are afraid of the consequences of real meditation. We do not wish to look into our basic attitudes to life, because it would be altogether too painful; it might well lead to the breaking up of our attachments, nay, the very destruction of the "me" as a separate entity. Not to nourish any longer the illusion of separateness, to give it all up and to acknowledge our nothingness, brings into being the fear of Death, death while still in the body; and this we cannot do. So we adjust to Society, which is much easier, much more in line with our usual activities, rather than adjust to Life, which is really no adjustment at all but a total negation—the negation of all socially imposed roles, of anything that has a cause and in itself serves as a further cause on the psychological plane, in this way maintaining limitation and so continuity for the ego.

Man in his utter nakedness unknowingly clings to the protection afforded by the incompleteness of his thought, which hides from him the fact of his nakedness and the complete meaninglessness of all social values and social morality. Thus the frantic activity of modern man is brought about because it serves as a giant escapism from facing the real facts of life: death, nothingness and, consequently, the insignificance of all his striving.

Conclusion

Having traveled to the end of the road, the truth has finally and suddenly emerged that, at least in principle, it is possible for a human mind to be truly free, even if nothing else in this world can be. We have come to this insight by understanding how man weaves the web of his continuity, which subjects him to the law of cause and effect. Since no one but himself is doing so, he is at liberty—once he is fully aware of this process—to stop it at any moment; as Krishnamurti once stated, "Man is his own liberator." But for this are needed more than good intentions: it requires a tremendous depth of understanding and an intense feeling of urgency that never dies. In the light of our discoveries the words of Ramana Maharshi acquire a new significance when he stated: "All the actions that the body is to perform are already decided upon at the time it comes into existence: the only freedom you have is whether or not to identify yourself with the body."

In pursuing our meditation to the very end we came across the clue, the very key to our freedom, contained in the understanding of continuity: the discovery of the mechanism governing the origination and the ending of thought. Once the whole sphere of ideation, the complete network of thought, is perceived, there is no longer a thinker—that is, thought has emptied itself, ended, and the conditioning background is destroyed. So, when the thought patterns which form our identity are exposed in their totality to awareness, thought is emasculated and unable to reproduce itself. Thought, which is a repetition of a pattern, no longer repeats, no longer creates images: in understanding, thought can only remain silent—this is the whole law. But how could it be otherwise, when the very birth of thought is occasioned by a lack of understanding of experience, by past action that is incomplete, by the not-seeing of the many contradictory desires that motivate and hold us.

So here is hope: in understanding the law, in the midst of the travails of everyday life, and especially then, there is a possibility—the *only* possibility—of breaking free from the clenched fist of determinism. There lies our opportunity to become truly human, and to cease being mechanical entities, condemned to act out unswervingly their destinies.

18

Some
Further
Reflections

Let us first find peace within ourselves before seeking peace with our environments.

We say, "Seeing is believing." To this writer, to see something truly, in its totality, means the very opposite: the freedom from every kind of belief, of speculation, and the end of dependence in any form.

All one's psychological problems are homemade.

Sexual morality (immorality) is relatively unimportant (harmless). What is important, however—very important

—is Morality. Let us sort out this one first, then the sexual morality will take care of itself.

Only the free mind is a happy mind. A mind desperately trying to be happy can never be free, being ever tethered to its projected goals; therefore it can never find happiness.

It is not the bare facts that disturb us, but thoughts about these facts. As long as there is agitation in the mind there can be no true perception, no proper understanding, of anything; and so long as understanding is lacking, there will be the intrusion of thought, the manufacture of illusion— a veritable vicious circle.

We cling to our memories, because there is no inward richness—they are all we have got, the nearest thing to permanency that man can attain.

Do not say: "This is good, that is bad . . . ," because it is a waste of time and energy—because while you do so you will never understand what you have so readily and smugly pigeonholed.
A man who has understood the things that really matter in life never labels his observations in this manner, nor does he nurture "likes" and "dislikes."

Does one ever take stock of one's life? Does one ever examine which activities are meaningful, and which are not? If one does, and begins to discover for oneself how much of one's life has no meaning at all, is a sheer waste of energy, then there will not even be any need to think of pruning one's activities. Then all the waste, all the noise, has already dropped away, and one finds oneself at once in a new way of life, infinitely more meaningful and more intense than the previous existence that had been taken so much for granted as being all there was to life.

The more insecure we feel, the more lost, the more ill adjusted to Life we are, the more we cherish the memories of past events, and the more associative thoughts based on the past intervene in our awareness of the present.

All one's problems, miseries, and moods of depression simply stem from the persistent pursuance of wrong (that is, unreal) values, and not from the lack of understanding of a philosophy or a religious doctrine.

The average man in bondage, when hit by misfortune, asks himself, "Why should this have happened to me?" Whereas the right question under the circumstances, asked by the man who is serious in his resolve to understand the roots of his bondage, would be, "Why should this not have happened to me?"—and when this man "meets with fortune," he asks himself, "Why should this have happened to me?" Thus both these questions could be part of an inquiry into what constitutes the entity to whom things happen. When the nature of this entity is perceived, or rather its nonnature, the happenings are transformed—they are seen to have been nonhappenings. This perception in its turn could lead to a way of functioning where sorrow no longer holds sway over our life.

The man who continues to be buffeted by Fate like a leaf before the wind never asks himself any vital questions and so never has an opportunity to break his bondage.

A sane society is ever essentially a moral society, but what is conventionally called a "moral society" is not a sane society.

Any conscious "religious" practice is not only unreal, but is immediately seized upon by the mind, which makes it into a refuge and therefore an escape. It blinds us to the necessity of understanding our day-to-day problems and activities. And if Religion does not give us an integral understanding of our daily life—which is the *only* life—what is its use?

We construct images about everything because the mind craves occupation, because we compare; we compare because we constantly measure ourselves: there is ever a space between the observer and the observed. We never observe from that Silence which is not the opposite of noise.

Is it not because we ever approach pleasure with an image (of what that pleasure should be, based upon the

174

memory of a previous experience) and therefore with an idea, that no pleasure can be simply experienced and dropped but always leads to a demand for further pleasure?

As long as Society is what it is, we shall have interminable problems. Society is not different from the individual, and the individual is not different from Society. The psychological structure of Society faithfully reflects the innermost thoughts of man. Those who postulate that the individual and Society are different entities have not thought out the issue properly. Also, it is comforting to perpetuate the split; it suits our psychological inertia, because in saying "Society must change" we absolve ourselves from the need to change as individuals.